# sacred
# stones
## and crystals

# sacred stones
## and crystals

*Connecting with the ancient wisdom
of stones, pebbles, and crystals*

Philip Permutt & Lyn Palmer

**CICO BOOKS**

LONDON NEW YORK

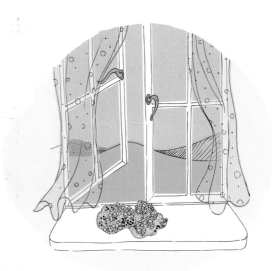

Published in 2011 by CICO Books
An imprint of Ryland Peters & Small Ltd

20–21 Jockey's Fields          519 Broadway, 5th Floor
London WC1R 4BW               New York, NY 10012

www.cicobooks.com

10 9 8 7 6 5 4 3 2 1

A CIP catalog record for this book is available from the Library of Congress
and the British Library.

ISBN: 978 1 907563 65 2

Printed in China

Editor: Marion Paull
Designer: David Fordham
Photographer: Roy Palmer
Illustrator: Trina Dalziel

# contents

Introduction 6

CHAPTER 1 Discover Sacred Stones 8

CHAPTER 2 Collecting Special Stones 28

CHAPTER 3 Rock Art 48

CHAPTER 4 Working with your Sacred Stones 64

CHAPTER 5 The Mystery of the Stones 80

CHAPTER 6 Medicine Bag: The Psychology of Stones 96

CHAPTER 7 An Introduction to Crystal Healing 112

Useful Resources 124

Index 125

Acknowledgments 128

# introduction

*hemimorphite*

Across the globe, many people have a natural fascination with stones of all shapes, sizes, and colors. We have all collected pebbles and stones that have caught our eye, picked them up, examined them, befriended them, and taken them home to make treasures of them. Who hasn't been fascinated by a crystal and amazed by an ancient sacred site? The innate energy of these stones somehow seems to draw us to them, and they have a direct effect on our feelings, whether we carry one in our pocket or they have been placed in special ways at celebrated places by different people from different cultures. Sometimes they just exist, creating a natural sacred space. By exploring this phenomenon, *Sacred Stones* takes you on a journey that can benefit your well-being on physical, emotional, and spiritual levels. It is a guide to discovering your personal connection to the world of stones, great and small.

Sacred stones are, in fact, all around us. Whether we notice them or not, they are part of, and enrich, our world—stones, rocks, crystals, and minerals that focus, store, transmit, and transmute energy. This applies just as much in the technologically driven 21st century as it has ever done. For example, electrical machines are guided by the piezo- and pyro-electrical properties of quartz crystal, which has been associated with ancient healing and mystical powers for millennia.

Since the dawn of mankind, stones and rocks have been revered throughout the world. Monumental structures, both natural and man made, were, and often still are, regarded as holy. From the stone circles at Avebury in England and the natural rock formation Uluru in Australia through the standing stones in the Côte des Megalithes in Brittany, France, and the

LEFT Sacred stones are all around us, from great monuments to pebbles on a beach, naturally cleansed by the waves.

petroglyphs etched on rocks in the Sonoran Desert in Arizona, USA to the crystal or pebble you carry in your pocket, stones are regarded as sacred. Stone lore and legends abound; perhaps the most famous sacred stones of all are the two tablets of lapis lazuli on which the Ten Commandments were written.

*rainbow fluorite*

At the other end of the spectrum, small stones and crystals have been used for healing and ceremony by medicine people and shamans for thousands of years. At Stonehenge, in England, a multitude

*lapis lazuli*

of small pebbles of blue Preseli stone from which the original monument was created, are believed to have been used for healing, possibly carried by people in need and placed on wounds or the chakras, the body's energy centers. The recorded use of small stones dates back over 5,000 years in Chinese and Indian texts, and even the Bible has over 200 references to crystals, minerals, and gemstones, as well as their powers and associations. Sacred stones have been found in prehistoric graves from the Olmec civilization in Central America to the pharaohs of ancient Egypt. The ancient Greeks were fascinated by the mystery of stones, and the great scientists Plato, Theophrastus, and Socrates all wrote on the subject.

There are many opinions about why sacred sites were built, and how crystals can heal, but in this book we concentrate on the stones themselves and the practical ways you can interact with them. Throughout, we interchange the words crystal, rock, stone, pebble, and mineral freely. Native Americans call these collectively the Stone People. They are part of our natural world, and they are ready to help us on our journey.

*various calcite crystals (clockwise from left):*
*orange, honey, green, dogtooth*

## Chapter 1

# Discover Sacred Stones

Discovering sacred stones for yourself can be a fascinating, life-long journey. Connect with stones at some of the world's most ancient sacred stone sites. As you find out more about stones both fixed and portable, great and small, see your own pathway of stones open up new possibilities from gazing in awe at them to working closely with their powerful energies.

# exploring sacred stone sites

*We are all fascinated by ancient sacred stone sites. Who built them? What was their purpose? Why did people take so much trouble to create them? Countless questions come to mind in their presence. The whole planet is filled with sacred stone sites, ranging in size from a few paces to many miles.*

We have chosen four ancient sites to show how you can connect with the stones, and use them to help with life's challenges—Avebury, Wiltshire, UK; Côte des Megalithes, Brittany, France; the Sonoran Desert, Arizona, USA; and Uluru, Australia.

The first step, however, is always to investigate local sites, whether a single stone, remnants of a henge or a ditch marking where a sacred shrine once stood, a church built over a holy well, or an international world heritage site—with a little research, you may be surprised to find an ancient sacred site almost on your doorstep. The exercises in this chapter can be practiced as described, or with small adaptations, at most sacred sites throughout the world.

## Avebury

*The largest and oldest stone circle in the world, Avebury is one of the most important Neolithic sites in Europe. It is about 5,000 years old and the perfect place to explore many of the activities you can try at your local sacred site.*

As you approach from the east, you come around a bend and, dramatically, arrive among the stones. Two stone circles, one inside the other, were built within a henge, which is a roughly circular bank and ditch. Stone burial barrows and manmade hills are part of the site, which is so large that it accommodates part of a village. A 1½-mile (2.5-km) avenue, 82ft (25m) wide, lined with large standing stones links the main stone circles with the Sanctuary, the site where a wooden circle once stood, on the outskirts of the sacred complex.

Many theories exist about the purpose of the Avebury site. Like most Neolithic henges with stone circles, much of the alignment is astronomical. Even the village church has been linked to the constellation Draco, with the depiction of a dragon on its font. Ancestor worship was common during much of the time when Avebury was being built and actively used, and the barrows, tumuli, and avenue suggest this was at least part of its purpose. We will probably never know the truth. The whole site, including the nearby manmade mound of Silbury Hill, which had a brilliant white finish when new, and the West Kennet long barrow just opposite, has been described as a "ritual-complex"—a place where many sacred sites interweave, possibly because of the natural formation of the countryside, created over many thousands of years.

## a stone's power

*I (Philip) once cast a crystal into the Kennet River, asking that a specific problem that was greatly troubling me at the time be removed from my life. It would have gone by itself in time, but I was amazed to find that it disappeared overnight and never affected me again. Whether this was psychological or the energy of the universe actually shifted, in a small way changing it, I may never know, but it doesn't matter because it worked. Try the following sequence to harness a stone's power:*

1 Select an object that represents the past issue that is hampering you. A crystal or a tumble-polished stone is fine, but you may also use a photo or an item that reminds you of a person or an event.

2 Go to the river and spend a little time by its bank. If possible, walk along beside it and cross to the other side so you can see different perspectives of the watercourse.

3 Find a place on the riverbank or on a bridge. Stay there quietly for a short time. Ask your spirit guide or angel guardian to help you. Focus your mind on the river, then on the issue that you want to discard.

4 When you feel ready—and this is a feeling, not timing, so it could be a few seconds or several hours—throw the object you are carrying into the river with the intent that the river, the gods, the universe, or whatever you believe is out there guiding your path through time and space, will take away the specific trouble, that it will not come back to you, and that it is null and void in your mind and in your heart.

5 Hold a moment of silence; perhaps thank your spirit guide or angel guardian and the gods for their help. Then carry on your normal everyday life and forget the whole thing. You will find that everything seems better in just a few days.

> Please be aware of your environment, and if you are going to cast an item into a river or leave anything at a sacred site, ensure that it is natural and/or biodegradable and will not harm the flora and fauna. If you prefer, you can imagine that you are throwing the object into the water and later discard it suitably.

## entering the stones

*The first time I (Lyn) experienced entering into a stone was a complete surprise and left me in a state of absolute awe and wonder. Philip and I love to walk around the massive stones at Avebury, and I am amazed anew every time we visit. I like to spend time with several stones if I can, just gazing at each one, then laying my hands on it, sensing the energies and feeling the antiquities the stone's surface emits. I have a favorite stone, which I always go to see.*

This particular time, I stopped off at "my" stone and Philip headed off to visit his own favorite stone. I spent some time with mine as usual, placing my hands on it and closing my eyes the better to sense the powerful energies emanating from deep within it. An impression of timelessness came over me as I idly mused on how many other hands had rested in that same place, and what thoughts had passed through those people's minds. At other times I have simply felt refreshed and contented, with a sense of well-being and a clearer mind. This time it was different.

As I leaned into the stone, wondering about those ancient people who had gone before me, I had a distinct sensation of a subtle shift, a feeling of actually entering into the stone—sensing the roughness of the stone's interior as I passed through the outer "wall," an awareness of damp, dark ancientness. It really felt as though I had penetrated completely into the very core of this stone. I wondered afterward if I had, in fact, disappeared from view for a few moments.

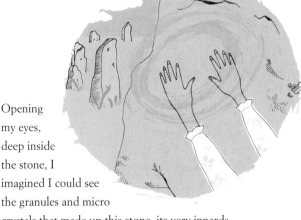

Opening my eyes, deep inside the stone, I imagined I could see the granules and micro crystals that made up this stone, its very innards. I was held securely in a time warp and noticed I was holding my breath. I didn't try to move because I did not want to break the moment of magic, although I was beginning to feel vague stirrings of unease and possibly panic rising. I fought it down, eager to prolong this incredible experience. I closed my eyes once more to concentrate and suddenly saw a hazy vision of the entire stone circle as it must have been in the earliest days, enshrouded in mist. Shadowy figures seemed to flit between the stones and mysterious faces came and went close by me. It lasted for a fleeting moment and I cannot be sure how much was my own imagination.

I found myself thinking about where Philip might be, because I would have liked to share the moment with him. I turned my head and took a step back. For a split second, there was a primitive roaring sound like a thousand voices, and then I found myself once again on the outside, with my hands still firmly planted on the surface of the stone.

I looked around, expecting Philip to have come looking for me, because, as I thought, I'd been such a long time, but there was no sign of him. I glanced at my watch and realized it had been only seven minutes since he left.

## connecting with the stones

*It may be that something will be revealed to you immediately during this exercise, or it may enter your mind at a later time. Have a notebook with you to record your experience, which will, of course, be unique.*

**1** When you come across one stone that, for you, stands out from the crowd, try to engage with it. Spend some time with that special stone you are drawn to. Perhaps sit facing it, or lean your back against it. After a while, go to the reverse side and do the same – how does that feel in comparison?

**2** When you feel ready, close your eyes, relax your mind from its everyday traffic, and allow the flow of random thoughts and feelings. You may feel yourself becoming deeply "joined" with this stone.

**3** When you feel you have connected in some way, and felt a response from the stone, stand up. Place both your hands at about chest height, flat onto the surface of the stone. Move your body and feet slowly forward until you have as much body contact with the stone as is comfortable. Wait. Be patient. Things do not necessarily happen in our perspective of time. Maybe nothing will happen. Still be patient. You may feel a subtle shift either physically or in your consciousness; you may feel a tingling sensation. Try not to analyze this, but allow yourself to enter into the experience with the stone more deeply. Feel and sense what is going on in and around you. Breathe. Enjoy your experience.

**4** When you feel ready, take a step back and break the moment. Reflect before you move on. You might also want to ground yourself (see page 17).

### links with a sacred river

The Kennet River, which flows through the Avebury site, is regarded as sacred by some people. The Druids used to cast items of value into rivers and lakes to appease the gods, or to ask for their support in a project or a challenge to come. The same can be done to remove problems you feel exist because of something that happened in the past.

## sacred sites through the ages

The Romans were perhaps the first to actively pursue a strategy of religious conversion of conquered peoples. Although they were regarded, by and large, as tolerant of other religious beliefs, they nevertheless needed the local population to be subdued. Weaning them away from their own gods was a good way of achieving this. To this end, they would either leave the local temple intact and merely add statues of their own gods, or they would extend the existing temple, or build a new one next to the local sacred site. In any case, the local people continued going to the same place to pray and would simply, by default, be praying to the Roman gods. When Christianity spread throughout Europe, the same thing happened, and as a result many old churches are built on ancient Pagan sacred sites.

# dowsing

*Every sacred site throughout the world is built where it is because people were drawn to the place by its natural energy and the conjunction of energy lines. For example, there's a church in Wheathampstead in Hertfordshire, England, where a number of lines clearly converge. Some of these are modern roads, but others are simply features in the landscape that are obvious in aerial photographs. The church, like many places of worship, probably stands on a previous sacred site.*

You can follow these lines of energy using any dowsing tool (see below), and dowsing is a perfect prehistoric practice to work with at an ancient sacred site. Many explanations of how dowsing might work have been put forward, but the most important thing is that it does work. We know this because all the water companies and oil companies in the world use professional dowsers, and they wouldn't be paying them if it didn't work!

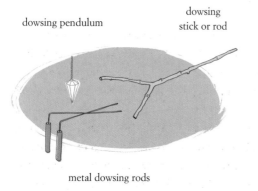

dowsing pendulum

dowsing stick or rod

metal dowsing rods

You can work with a pendulum or dowsing rods. A crystal pendulum is easier when you start because the crystal helps to focus the energy. Dowsing rods are made from a forked twig or branch, or you can buy metal ones.

1 Tune in to your dowser. If you are using a pendulum, hold its chain or thread and ask it a simple question, such as, "Am I a woman?" The pendulum will move back and forth, right to left, in clockwise or counter-clockwise circles. Then ask, "Am I a man?" Your dowsing pendulum will move in a different way. These are your "yes" and "no" answers.

2 With dowsing rods or sticks, place a coin on the ground. From a few yards away, walk toward it with the dowsing device held loosely but securely in front of you. With a little practice you'll find a comfortable way of holding them. Focus your mind on the idea of finding money. When the dowsing rods pass over the coin, they will move, either together or apart. If you have a forked stick, it will move up or down.

## following energy lines

*It takes time and practice, but it is possible to map the energy lines of an entire site for yourself. At Avebury, by following just a few energy lines through the site you will see that the original placement of the stones some 5,000 years ago was not random, but calculated to mirror the natural energies within the land.*

1 Choose a standing stone and map it with your dowsing tool. To do this, dowse the area immediately around the base of the stone. You will find more energy being emitted in some directions than in others, as if the stone is "pointing" in those directions.

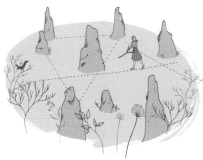

2 With your back to the stone, starting at one of the strong energy points, use your dowsing tool to follow the line on the ground as far as you can. This will often take you straight to another stone or to a place where a stone used to stand. At Avebury, this is easy because stations where stones once stood are marked with small concrete posts, which is not always the case elsewhere. You may need to look for dips or raised areas on the ground to identify where standing stones once were. They may have fallen and been covered, so are now underground.

## grounding

If you have difficulty tuning into your dowsing instrument, you probably need grounding. When you are holding a pendulum, the simplest thing to do is to hold a hematite stone in your other hand. If you have dowsing rods or sticks, put the hematite stone in your pocket or bra. This will help to ground you, creating a foundation for energy to flow through you and convert into the movement of your dowsing tool.

Other ways to ground yourself include clapping your hands, stamping your feet, drinking a reasonable quantity of water, and eating a few cookies.

## asking the stones for help

*For thousands of years, people have traveled to sacred sites to ask for help, healing, or success. Astrological alignments at Avebury suggest that all the major seasonal festivals were celebrated among the stones, and the summer and winter solstices, in particular, still are. However, many people make a solo pilgrimage when they feel like it, or go as a tourist to find that, unexpectedly, one stone in particular pulls them near.*

1 Stand still in front of your chosen stone and focus on your crown chakra, at the top of your head (see page 119).

2 Slowly allow your attention to move down your body to your feet. Imagine your feet sinking into the ground right by your stone, and as they sink, you connect in the ground with your stone in front of you.

3 Place your hands on the stone, make your request, and when you have finished, thank your stone as if it has already completed the task you have set it. If you have brought a small offering—something natural is most suitable—put it at the foot of, or on, the stone.

The Kerlescan alignments are open during the off season only, and you may not be able to gain access to the stones at other times. The season generally runs from May 1 to September 30, but check before you visit.

# Côte des Megalithes

*This is the largest Neolithic site in Europe, covering about 15 miles (24km) of the Brittany coast in and around the town of Carnac, in France. One of the major Celtic centers in the world, the site has 3,000 standing stones, mostly arranged in avenues, but also dolmens and tumuli (tombs) and menhirs (single standing stones).*

Holy wells are now often surmounted by churches, and some of the standing stones have been removed or knocked over, while others have had crosses added to them; but despite the Christianization of the region, the site is still clear to see and experience.

Many different legends are associated with these stones, ranging from them being a Roman legion turned to stone by the great Celtic wizard Merlin, to a Pope working the same magic on Pagan warriors who were chasing him. One story describes them as Roman tent pegs (for some very large tents!) Thousands of Christian saints are associated with the area, each with a tale attached, often detailing how the saint mystically acquired the powers of a pre-existing Pagan god. Folktales of nature spirits and faeries, and of King Arthur and Merlin, abound. These stories are often contradictory and serve more to confuse than enlighten us.

The reasons for the massive effort and organization needed to create these sites have been questioned for hundreds of years and are still debated today. As with other Neolithic stones, one idea is that Carnac was an astronomical observatory. Alignments with the sunset at the solstices are in evidence, and more recent studies have shown other astrological orientations. Links to various death cults have been suggested, due to the large number of dolmens and tumuli, but the most likely answer is that it was associated with ancestor worship, which was generally practiced in Neolithic times throughout northern Europe.

## bearing gifts

I (Philip) like to give my special stone a gift of a small crystal after asking for its help with whatever issue I may have to address at that time.

Some people wonder why I leave a crystal, thinking someone might take it. There is a Native American philosophy that the gift is in the giving, and this I believe. Once the gift has been given, nothing else matters. You can give a prized possession to a young child who breaks it instantly, but the gift was in the moment of giving. Crystals have a value to me, sometimes well beyond their commercial worth. So I choose to give a crystal to mark the event as something special, perhaps sacred. As for it being "stolen"—if the sacred stone it's been given to chooses to give it away once I've gone, who am I to argue with it?

## welcoming the sun into your day

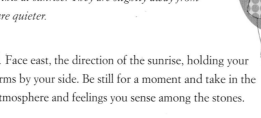

*The avenues of stones at the Kerlescan alignments, or the remains of the stone circle at the western end of the alignments, are a good place to try this at sunrise. They are slightly away from the main site, and so are quieter.*

**1** Face east, the direction of the sunrise, holding your arms by your side. Be still for a moment and take in the atmosphere and feelings you sense among the stones.

**2** As the sun starts to rise, lift your arms away from your sides, palms facing forward, and bring them up over your head, so the fingertips of each hand are touching. You may feel the sun's energy in the open palms of your hands; if not, imagine it.

**3** When you feel your hands are full with sunlight, bring them down together in front of you to your solar plexus and imagine the sunlight from your hands entering your body. Your solar plexus is the center where you store energy to use later in the day.

**4** Repeat this three times, or more if you like, until you feel fully charged with the sacred energy of the Carnac stones, and ready to face the day.

## walking meditation

*It is best to do this by the remains of the stone circle at the western end of the Kerlescan alignments.*

1 Walk slowly east through the avenues of stones. The standing stones line up in 13 ranks for about half a mile. As you walk, notice each step you take. Be aware of the stones around you and the ground beneath you.

2 Allow yourself to feel a connection to each stone as you pass it, and if you feel drawn to a particular stone, spend some time with it.

3 Continue this exercise for as long as you wish, but if you have limited time, it may be a good idea to set some sort of alarm, perhaps on your mobile phone. Otherwise, you could find yourself still tuning in to individual standing stones at dusk!

## contacting the ancestors

*This exercise is best done early or late in the day, when there are fewer people around.*

1 Choose one of the several dolmens or tumuli accessible in the area. Sit on the ground inside the tomb, close your eyes, and for a while imagine how dark it would be when it was originally sealed. The stones making up the tomb would have been covered with earth.

2 Focus your mind on the "Old Ones," the ancient people, the ancestors who built these monuments. Take your time and slowly check in with each of your senses. Notice what you see in your mind's eye, what you hear, and any aromas that may waft by. Be aware of how the ground feels beneath you and any flavors that activate the taste buds on your tongue.

3 Follow whichever of your senses is responding best to the stimuli, and listen with your heart to any "voices," however they come to you. Perhaps you will find the answer to something that is worrying you, or information concerning one of your own ancestors. Probably, you will have a deeper connection than before to the ancient Celts, or to even earlier civilizations of the region.

4 When you are ready, gradually allow yourself to become aware of your body. Notice each of your senses in turn and slowly open your eyes, bringing your senses back to the present inside your stone tomb.

# petroglyphs of the Sonoran Desert

*Petroglyphs are images carved or etched in stone—the word comes from two Greek words, petros meaning "stone" and glyphein "to carve." They can be drawings of objects and events, such as animals and hunts; or symbols, pictograms representing groups of words, and ideograms representing ideas or concepts, such as gods and religious beliefs.*

 Petroglyph sites are sacred and rare. Please do not climb on the rocks or damage them in any way. Take nothing from the area and leave nothing that you have brought.

Petroglyphs have been found on every continent where humans have lived. Along with cave paintings, they are the original form of rock art.

It is very difficult to estimate the age of these rock carvings. Firstly, the rocks themselves are millions of years old, and secondly, there is often a fine film of microbes giving color to the etched surface, which may, when age tested, show results suggesting some petroglyphs were created yesterday! By comparing them to styles of decoration on pottery and other artefacts, which are dateable, conventional estimates put the oldest petroglyphs at 10–12,000 years old. Other sources suggest that the oldest petroglyphs may have been found in Bhimbetka, central India. These are conservatively dated to 290,000 BCE but recent discoveries suggest they may be as old as 700,000 BCE. Either of these ages pre-date modern humans, who evolved around 200,000 years ago.

There is great debate about the meanings and purpose of petroglyphs. Were they early art, or teaching aids, or even history lessons? Some seem to be depictions of actual events, such as a specific hunt, while others may appear to be similar at first until we notice a mythical creature. Did these creatures once exist or are they part of a belief system being deliberately passed on through art to future generations? Perhaps some petroglyphs were maps, possibly to direct bands of hunter-gatherers to either the next waterhole or to the next life. The biggest problem is that modern interpretations of petroglyphs tell us more about the psychology of current observers than about the people who created them or their intended meanings. It has also been suggested that the designs seen in ancient rock art are locked within our psyche and can be easily recreated by young children at play. Another idea is that perhaps they are designs from a shamanic culture, and the only way to understand them is to enter a trance to alter our state of consciousness. Whatever the case, these enigmatic symbols from our past are intriguing.

The petroglyphs in the Sonoran Desert are mostly carved by the Hohokam people. Hohokam means "those who have vanished" in Pima, a local Native American language. They inhabited the area between 350 BCE and AD 1450, and then simply disappeared.

## sacred moment at Signal Hill

Signal Hill is quite a small location and is completely visible from a small mound nearby. Art—a Native American who was guiding us through the sacred history of his people in the area—Lyn and I were standing on the mound. Each of us was facing a different direction, one toward the petroglyphs and the other two toward the Sonoran Desert with its giant Saguaro cacti. For a very long moment—it could have been minutes or hours—we just stood there in the silence, connecting to the ancient sacredness of the place and to each other. The feeling was timeless.

## connecting with the universe

*You can achieve this indescribable feeling by yourself or in small groups of up to four. Each person stands facing one of the cardinal directions.*

**1** Breathe slowly, but naturally, and focus your mind on your breathing. Follow your breath as you breathe in and keep following it, imagining that your breath is flowing through your body to your feet.

**2** Notice your feet on the ground. Realize that you are standing on a sacred spot, a place where people have stood for thousands of years.

**3** Look in front of you into the distance. Know in this moment that you are connected to all that you see and that, in turn, this is connected to everything else in the universe. Be with these thoughts; you will know when it is time to stop.

Petroglyphs may be seen in the caves, overhangs, and rock shelters at Uluru, including on the Mala and Mutitjulu walks. See page 22 for more on petroglyphs.

## what do petroglyphs mean to you?

*This exercise is may help you to find a deeper understanding of your worries and concerns.*

**1** Draw a copy of any petroglyph image you choose. Focus on the original image in the rock and next to your drawing write the first word that comes into your mind, and then any others. Repeat this process for as many petroglyphs as you can see.

**2** When you have finished, look at your drawings and words. Is there a consistency in the meanings of similar designs? Note whether you have given mostly physical or metaphysical answers. Be aware of any sentences you are forming, either in your interpretation or through the order in which you have chosen to explore the petroglyphs.

### ancient wisdom

It's amazing how accurately ancient stories from many cultures reflect current scientific knowledge. Most stories of Uluru's creation revolve around wars between "ancestor beings" or "ancestor spirits." All involve these beings traveling, destroying, and creating the landscape as we see it today, just like the upheavals caused by volcanic activity and sea-level changes that scientists use to explain our environment. The Anangu, traditional landowners of this sacred site, believe that the land is still inhabited by the ancestors.

# Uluru

*Situated more or less at the center of Australia is a massive red sandstone rock, almost 6 miles (more than 9km) around the base and 1,100 ft (335m) high. Uluru (Ayers Rock) is perhaps the most sacred and mystical place on the whole continent, and certainly one of its most recognizable images.*

Uluru holds deep significance for the Pitjantjatjara—the local aboriginal people, who call themselves Anangu—who believe it was created in the Dreamtime, when everything came into being. The ancestors created all things, including the current landscape. The Dreamtime refers to the past, the present, and the future, how they interact and everything they encompass.

RIGHT Uluru at sunrise and
sunset, when the rock
glows a stunning red,
is an amazing sight. The
colors change from
grays to browns to reds to
oranges and yellows as
the light alters.

## walking to find the Dreamtime

*Most of the official recommended activities at
Uluru involve walks. The Pitjantjatjara believe that
true spiritual experience comes from listening to
everything while you are walking. Take the traditional
route circumnavigating the base of Uluru. You are
asked not to climb the rock as it is a sacred site and
the tourist path, with chain handhold, crosses a sacred
Dreamtime track.*

The Anangu are the traditional landowners and
offer small, exclusive group tours that give
fascinating insights into aboriginal history, culture,
and traditions. Many Dreamtime legends are
associated with natural features in the area and the
travels of the ancestral heroes through the land.
Special rocks, caves, sand hills, and sacred groves
have their own Dreamtime tales to tell.

# Kata Tjuta

*Another astonishing rock site, about 19 miles (30km) away from Uluru,
and 656ft (200m) higher, Kata Tjuta comprises 36 vaguely rounded domes
of rock. The name means "many heads" in the local aboriginal language.
It is formed of conglomerate rather than sandstone, and walking there
generally follows one of two main routes.*

Many Dreamtime stories relate to Wanambi, the
great snake king, who is reputed to live on the
highest summit, Mt Olga. His rainbow colors
support his life-giving gifts. Perhaps he sleeps in the
mud of a drying riverbed or waterhole in the dry
season, resting so he can fly in the sky as a rainbow
sending down waters from the sky in the rainy
season. His breath is the wind.

   Most Dreamtime legends are still closely guarded
secrets, and although Kata Tjuta is used by local
people for ceremonies, most are conducted at night
and in their own secret world.

## Chapter 2

# Collecting Special Stones

This chapter introduces you to some of our own special stones, how we acquired them, what they mean to us, and how we work with them; also what it is that gets us all stone-spotting, and discovering the sacredness within each stone. We hope that this will inspire you to start, or continue to build, your own collection, taking a fresh look at getting the best out of your stones, and entice you to explore new ways of enjoying them as well as working with them.

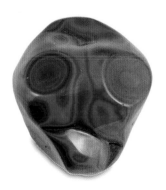

# pebble hunting

*When you are idly walking along a pebbly beach, has a stone ever caught your eye? One particular stone—doesn't seem to be a reason—just waves up from the multitude. Or when you look down, have you seen a face shining up at you? It could be a smiley, friendly face, or one that is a bit grim and scary, or even comical.*

Occasionally, you can pick up a stone that has a clear face, with all the features defined, but by the time you get it home the face is lost and you're not able to see it. Maybe it just served its purpose—to cheer you up, to warm you, to make you laugh, or to remind you of someone or something, transmitting healing energy or perhaps a timely warning. But the moment has passed and as much or as often as you look, the face eludes you. If this happens, put the stone back or give it to a friend. In some small way it has helped you and now needs to serve someone else.

We can never know how long a stone has remained unnoticed, or how many different people have made a treasure of it, or even a weapon. Maybe someone carried it for a few days, added it to a collection, discarded it, or carried it for a lifetime. How much of the essence or the energy of a person, place, or event has been captured into that stone, and passed on for good or evil to the next custodian?

So whenever you're out pebble hunting or just walking, if you're drawn to a particular stone, remember that there's usually a reason. There's no need to try to work out why immediately; just notice the stone and it may become obvious to you. Pick up the stones you're drawn to and be aware of any similarities in shape, color, texture, and feelings they evoke within you. A pattern may start to emerge as the stones try to tell you what you need to know at this time.

Stones may be visibly pleasing or arresting or even disconcerting. They are tactile and some seem to fit into your hand as though they belong there. Others may well have been important in the past, not necessarily in their own right but as part of something else—perhaps a corner stone, a stone someone was trying to carve, a flint tool, or a flying chip from a mason's chisel as he fashioned an angel or a gargoyle. Each stone takes on and holds energy from whoever possesses and interacts with it, and from that person's intention, and this energy may stay within the stone for hours, days, weeks, months, years, or even for centuries.

# where to find your sacred stones

*You can pick up pebbles, stones, rocks, and crystals from numerous places. More are to be found in the natural environment than you might think. A rummage in your back yard, or a garden, riverbank, or disused quarry will produce many different crystals in most areas.*

Especially good places to look are beaches and watercourses, such as a stony stream bed. Pebbles found in these places often seem as though they have been polished because they have been worn smooth by the stream or the sea. Sometimes they even have a shiny finish. These are known as alluvial crystals.

Of course, you can buy crystals online or from a crystal, rock, or new-age shop. Each stone has a special quality—for example amethyst, which can relieve headaches, and flint, which can help to calm arguments and stop nightmares. Crystal healers have

*alluvial topaz crystals*

been helping people for thousands of years with stones and their healing properties. So when you next go into a crystal shop, be open to and aware of the stones, and listen for the one that's calling to you.

---

### Lyn's uvarovite

I have a lovely piece of this green crystalline variety of garnet. Before I knew what it was and where it had come from, I took a shine to it, enjoying the feeling of the tiny crystals on its rough surface under my fingertips. It was a hot summer's day and I closed my eyes and began to meditate. I was soon transported to a desolate wasteland, frozen, and bitterly cold with a chill wind. It was quite overwhelming. I told Philip about it and he said, "Well, it *does* come from Siberia!" So the uvarovite was telling its own stony story of its past.

*uvarovite*

All stones have a metaphysical value, and it doesn't matter if you've bought them in a shop or picked them up at the side of the road; this value has nothing to do with money. Some stones that we've picked up over the years we just wouldn't part with. When you spend any length of time with crystals—the Stone People (see page 86)—you find that they come in and out of your life like friends. Some pass through, others are lifelong. They have colors, patterns, shapes, and feelings that we are drawn to, that we notice and find pleasing. Sometimes a pattern emerges in our selections. All the stones may be blue or have wavy lines or pointed ends or feel smooth. There is always a reason, and for now it is enough just to recognize that this happens. (See Chapter 6 for more details.) If you already have a collection of stones, why not take a moment to have a look through it and see if you can identify any recurring patterns in the stones you select.

## negative energy

A jeweler friend made three stunningly beautiful and amazingly expensive necklaces from diamonds and rubies over a period of several days. When they were finished, he sent them to three different stores and two sold within a couple of weeks. After six months the third had still not sold and he asked us about this. Although all three were unique designs, they were in the same style, made from the same gemstones from the same source, and all of the same high quality. A little investigation produced the information that many people had liked the look of the final necklace in the store, but everyone who had asked to have a closer look had said, "It's beautiful, but I don't like the feel of it," or, "It doesn't feel right." We asked him if he remembered anything about this necklace and one of the things that stuck in his mind was that he had had a row with his wife the morning he finished this one. He had obviously been very upset by the argument and we suggested that this negative energy had been locked into the gemstones as he finished his work. We recommended he cleansed the necklace thoroughly (see page 118), which he did and returned it to the same shop where it sold within a couple of weeks.

## trust the stones

When I (Philip) had my own shop, it never ceased to amaze me that regular customers would come in and be drawn to different types of crystal each time. I was, too. Every day a different crystal would catch my eye. As I worked more and more with crystals, I found that people were drawn to the one they needed at that particular time. Some can even be predictive, so it may not be obvious why you are drawn to a stone. Perhaps you will need it in the near future—for travel plans, possibly, or for a significant life change. And you may be attracted to a crystal when you are thinking about someone else.

# our special stones

*Among all the many stones that we have encountered over the years in various parts of the world, certain ones stand out. They are our special crystals and they stay with us, working and sometimes playing, and often teaching us along the way. Lending their various qualities to all sorts of situations, both everyday and exceptional, they have become firm and dependable friends. Some of these crystals we bring out as and when they are needed, but many are always within reach or sight; they are part of our lives, almost like family.*

We especially love the ones that wear their own individual faces on their surfaces. Expressions and characters of all kinds appear to catch our initial attention, to make us take notice of them. It is as if they are letting us know that they have something unique to bring us to assist with our diverse intentions and goals. Faces often appear in much bigger stones, too—standing stones, pavement stones, walls, buildings. We've seen stones whose faces appear animated. Is it the light changing subtly, or a message, or the stone just being itself? Why do some stones have human faces, some animal, and some distinctly alien? Others are like trapped emotions—Edvard Munch's "The Scream" (see opposite) is reproduced in an agate we have. Did these stones witness something? Some of them seem to be watching us sternly, and we catch sight of their disapproving faces when we are about to do something, well, mischievous. Others almost give a nod of approval, inspiring and encouraging.

Some of our special stones are the ones that have found a purpose in life—at least in our life for the time being. These purposes vary from helping us to be creative, healing ourselves and others, teaching in classes, and for inspiration of all kinds—the list is long. We never know whether a stone will stay with us for ever or leave abruptly; it could be lost or given away. Of course, over the period of their lifetime, which is considerably longer than ours, stones may work with many different people on countless projects, perhaps lying dormant, either hidden from view or just unnoticed, perhaps on a beach. So we tend to treat all our special stones as very precious gems and appreciate all they contribute.

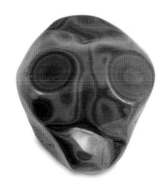

### Malachite Alien

When I (Lyn) first met my malachite alien, I definitely found him (yes, it's male) disconcerting. The way his large, concentric-circle-shaped eyes, created from his botryoidal structures in some ancient time, bored into mine was as if he knew all my secrets. I'm sure I stepped back a pace. Perhaps the malachite energy went directly to my heart chakra. I was definitely drawn to his green strangeness, but he soon gave me a calm, relaxed feeling.

As I spent time looking at him, I noticed his mouth turned down a little, giving him a slightly more approachable, even vulnerable, look. Sometimes it was pulled down in indecision. We connected. I learned that stern people have a vulnerable side. I also learned that it's okay to be different. I often sit and consult him when I'm contemplating a new venture, especially when I'm looking for ideas that are a bit off the wall, maybe slightly alien in nature.

### Agate Scream

When my son and I (Lyn) saw this crystal for the first time, we both exclaimed "The Scream," it so much reminded us of Edvard Munch's disturbing painting. It was such a sad and distraught face I wanted to cry for his pain. I thought I'd best leave him where he was, because it felt as though I would be courting negativity to bring him home, but of course I could not leave him.

I'm so glad, because looking at those distressed features reminds me that often people need compassion, which sometimes needs a kick-start when we're becoming a little too complacent. How easy it is to create a hurt look in someone's face, but how easy it is to remove it.

Agate promotes relationships, and can also help to protect us from lack of compassion in others.

### Hemimorphite

She (yes, it's a girl!) reminds me (Lyn) that beauty isn't always apparent. The lopsided grin and bulging eyes just have such great character. She looks as if she is about to tell a wonderful joke. She also reminds me to take care of my teeth—a good one to pocket when on the way to the dentist's. The color is beautiful, which is lovely to focus on when I need calming. She brings me both courage and inner contentedness.

Hemimorphite is a crystal that makes you feel better and brings luck and creativity.

## Amethyst Madonna

She is a wonderful touchstone who has been with me (Lyn) seemingly for ever. Just her simple presence is comforting, and the feel of the contours of the crystal around the thumb brings calm reassurance. This is one stone I keep tabs on. I always like to know where she is, and feel uneasy if I don't, in which case I have to make a rather obsessive search for her. This is odd since I'm not a compulsive person by nature. Other stones hide for a while, but I am always confident that they will reappear.

Amethyst does help with all forms of compulsive behavior. The shaping and gentle, subtle face gives the impression of a woman looking down at a baby in her arms. I call her my Madonna. She brings reassurance and strength.

Amethyst promotes calm, boosts you both emotionally and physically, and offers a different way of seeing your spiritual side.

## Orbicular Jasper

I (Lyn) love this one—so like the sea with his wave-crested hair and sandy eyes and mouth. It's strange, whenever I feel myself longing to be near the sea (which is often) and it's not possible to go there, I find myself drawn to this stone, moving him with me from room to room, touching and even sniffing him to reach the essence of the sea. He always brings happiness and soothes the longing. Like the sea itself, orbicular jasper helps calm emotions, and also promotes meditation and cleansing detox. He lives in the bathroom mostly.

## Brazilian Agate

This agate is a bit of a specter—no mouth, but big eyes. He sees everything yet speaks no evil. A protective crystal, he is a good stone to keep around or to take to meetings if I (Lyn) feel I might say too much or the wrong thing! Like all Brazilian agates, this one supports my intuition when I'm unsure of people around me. He can also evoke feelings for lost or homeless souls, galvanizing me into action in some way to alleviate suffering, or just to donate some things to charity.

## Fulgurite Man

His grumpy face sometimes sits on my laptop when I'm (Philip) writing, bringing flashes of inspiration and humor when the dreaded writer's block attempts to raise its head above the parapet. He reminds me to laugh at myself and not to take myself too seriously.

Created by lightning strikes on desert sands, which fuse quartz together from silicates, fulgurite is formed in the explosive world of nature and has the strength to blast blocks aside. Fulgurite also helps to increase concentration, and aids communication, making it a perfect ally for anyone trying to be creative.

## Amethyst Bearded Sailor

He reminds me (Philip) of the wise old man of the sea, and just like the mariner, this bearded amethyst crystal cluster has ancient wisdom and magical skills to draw upon. Comparable to the legends of the ancient Greek god Poseidon, he calms the waters after a storm; holding this crystal brings a sense of peace and tranquility. Sometimes he produces answers to questions I didn't know I wanted to ask.

Amethyst is a multipurpose crystal, helping with all sorts of things, but I feel this one works in the emotional world. Specifically, this crystal gives the impression of wanting to balance emotions, ease stress, and aid the natural flow of energy. The photograph shows what most people would call the back of the crystal.

## Metamorphosis Quartz

This is the greatest bringer of change in the crystal world, and all change is for the good, even if it feels uncomfortable while you are going through it. I (Philip) love the way that I can look into this crystal and see different scenes. They seem to change constantly, as the light shifts or I move the stone by an unnoticed fraction. It is as if a misty veil is covering a mountain so that I can see just a part of the vision and am never quite sure of the outcome, but I can see enough to know I'm following the right path.

Metamorphosis quartz is good for stimulating mental awareness and bringing positivity to your thoughts.

## Tibetan Smoky Quartz

This is one amazing crystal! An elestial crystal, a faden crystal, a rainbow crystal, and an etched crystal all in one! It fits perfectly in my (Philip's) hand, almost disappearing in my palm, with finger grips matching my right hand as if custom made. This is a protective crystal, giving advance warning of danger or troubles.

Elestial crystals have many points making up a termination, and point to the many possibilities we encounter on our path through life and the choices we face along the way. Smoky quartz elestial crystals specifically bring a positive outlook to our view of the road ahead. Faden crystals appear to have a white line running through them, but on closer inspection this is found to be a hollow tube, which acts as a bridge between people—a healer and his or her client, a shaman guiding someone on a journey.

"Rainbow" is a name given to many types of crystal that have no association with each other, which can cause confusion. This one has a natural rainbow inside the crystal, where light reflects though a fracture in the crystalline structure and brings inspiration. Etched crystals have markings along one or more sides that can resemble writing or hieroglyphs. They help us connect to our past.

Tibetan quartz crystals help us connect spiritually to the world around us and cut through mystical waffling, getting straight to the point.

## Talking Crystal

This double-terminated quartz crystal has been with me (Philip) since 1993. It's been in every class I've taught and every lecture I've given. The idea comes from the Native American concept of a talking stick; the stick is passed around the room, each person in turn having their chance to talk without interruption while they hold it. Some traditions say that you must speak the truth or the curse of the stick will get you! My crystal is not cursed, but it does do strange things—getting hot or cold, vibrating, and causing unusual sensations in people's heart or solar plexus as they hold it and talk. It has a green chlorite phantom at one end that helps you to see hidden answers. Really it helps my students to express the truth that is in their hearts.

## Tourmaline Teddy Bear

I'm (Philip) never quite sure if this is a teddy bear or a tree spirit. The fibrous schorl (black tourmaline) shimmers as I move the crystal in the light, a little like the patterns light might make dappling through the leaves of a tree, and he stands in a slightly lopsided way on the bedside table. He is joyous, a real "feel better" stone, always helping me to see the funny side of life.

Schorl aids creativity and practicality, and helps to relieve anxiety. It is also a grounding stone. This one makes me feel like my feet are tree roots, pushing into the earth. Again this is suggesting the tree connection, but I just love the idea of a tourmaline teddy bear.

## Aquamarine Crystal Cluster

This is another crystal I've (Philip) had for many years that helps with my teaching. She is full of mystery and surprise. As I turn her in the light, I find more and more hidden within her crystalline structure. To me, she represents the flow of universal energy through the room as I teach, and helps the interconnection between all the participants. She really helps me to communicate clearly, especially in expressing answers to unexpected questions that arise.

Aquamarine is very calming and gives protection to travelers on any journey, no matter how long or short.

## Quartz Crystal

This is my special crystal, which I (Philip) work with for healing only, either for my clients or for myself. It has been with me since I started as a crystal healer, and since it is cleansed (see page 118) between every client, it is the most purified crystal I know! This crystal can look quite dull sitting on a table or on a shelf, but as soon as I pick it up—wow! Rainbows appear and it sparkles and shines in the light. It just loves working and it knows where it needs to be. The crystal will often mysteriously guide my hand so that I'm holding it over a different part of a client's body, and it's always right. The client needs healing in this new area. (See Chapter 7 for basic crystal healing techniques.)

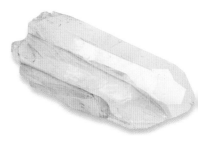

## CITRINE CRYSTALS

Citrine is one of my favorite types of crystal. A golden-colored form of quartz, it has a multitude of helpful habits from speeding healing after operations to bringing abundance and wealth.

## Citrine Writing Stone

This is a crystal I (Philip) was drawn to, so I took him home and placed him on a shelf, and nothing happened for many years until I received my first book contract. Suddenly, he almost launched himself from shelf to desk and now he lives next to my laptop whenever I'm writing. Among citrine's many properties are that it aids creativity and writing.

## Citrine Healing Stones

These three crystals have helped with my (Philip's) personal healing over the years. The top one found me (sometimes crystals choose you rather than you selecting them) when I first became interested in alternative therapies. It helped me greatly when I was seriously ill. The second one is a perfect thumb stone, with a very strokeable depression. The third is an unpolished double-terminated crystal from Tibet. All three of these stones have stunning rainbows within their structures.

Citrine helps with all sorts of conditions, including all bowel and digestive problems, nausea, weight loss and weight gain, detox, and anaemia.

## Citrine Till Crystal

This crystal has been sitting on the till in my (Philip's) shop since 1993 when I first entered the rock business. The till was made in the 1800s. It came from my father's shop and was my grandmother's before that. I added the citrine crystal. Whenever we had a quiet day in the shop, I'd rub this crystal and within minutes customers would come in, the phones would ring, and the computer would "ping" with another internet order. The crystal is a twin—two crystals naturally growing together. It has beautiful rainbows, but also iron inclusions giving discoloration in the smaller crystal, which just goes to show that everything does not always have to be perfect.

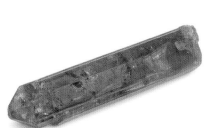

## Butterfly Rock

The butterfly represents transformation or change. It has the ability to metamorphose from a grubby chrysalis into a beautiful adult. This "stone" is a slice of petrified or fossilized wood. On one side is depicted a butterfly and on the other the head of a bear or perhaps a dog. These patterns were created completely naturally during the fossilization process.

This is a more recent acquisition and reminds me (Philip) that things are not always as they appear, and there are at least two sides to any story. It helps me to look for deeper meanings. Petrified wood assists this because it helps you to sort things out in your mind and grounds you, thereby relieving stress.

## Watermelon Tourmaline Crystal

This is another "feel better" stone that helps me (Philip) to connect to my higher self and see the funny side of situations. Just carrying it in a pouch or my pocket brings me a protective and loving energy that feels like I'm being cuddled and snuggled by a rather large and slightly slobbery dog. But don't be fooled by crystals that feel like this, because it's fiercely protective and it will bite anyone who ventures too close uninvited.

The deep pink running through the center of the crystal connects with the heart, balancing the emotions. Tourmaline helps to focus the mind.

## The Manifestation Egg

This is one of those crystals that comes around once in a lifetime— a crystal completely contained within another crystal. In this case, it's a fluorite crystal within a quartz crystal, which has been shaped in the form of an egg. The quartz also has fine rutile crystals growing through it. I (Philip) look at this crystal and disappear into it—lost, and at the same moment finding something new each time I venture within the stone.

Rutilated quartz is also known as "angel hair" and aids communication with our spirit guides and angels. Fluorite helps us to focus our minds, and clear fluorite in particular links our physical experiences with spiritual understanding. The manifestation crystal makes things happen; when everything seems stuck, as if your battery is flat, it can jump-start your motor.

### Blue Quartz Crystal

This is another crystal of transformation. It seems to point, like a sign on a highway, in the direction I (Philip) need to go. It takes me along a metaphysical path that allows me to leave old issues behind, and at the same time keeps me grounded and safe. Things I no longer need can be shed, like a butterfly shedding its chrysalis and emerging anew. The indicolite (blue tourmaline) crystals running through the quartz remind me of paths connecting to everyone I know, of spirits, and the universe. This is another crystal that feels as if it's made for my hand. It also has the formation of a scepter crystal, which can help things flow when I'm feeling stuck and don't know which way to go. A wonderful signpost stone.

### Herkimer Diamonds

When I (Philip) teach Reiki, these four Herkimer diamond crystals join me in the attunement space. This type of crystal helps people to tune into different vibrations of energy. I find they increase the experience of my students and help me to connect them to the Reiki energy. I may place them under chairs or in their hands; sometimes I like to have four chairs facing the cardinal directions with the crystals under them. Herkimer diamonds also promote new beginnings and psychic abilities, so are the perfect crystals to include in any ceremony from Reiki attunement to a formal wedding.

### Alien Animal Rock

This strange animal rock looks as though it has come from another planet. It did! It's a small Nantan meteorite that fell to earth in China in 1516, so it is, in fact, alien—part of Mars, blasted from the red planet's surface some five hundred years ago. It bears some resemblance to a Chinese lucky three-legged toad, a pig crossed with a dog, and a stegosaurus. I (Philip) feel he's one of nature's unique creations and he makes me smile, reminding me that there is beauty in everything. He helps me connect to my past. Sometimes he seems to bring me luck; at other times he just seems to need dusting. He's always happy to help with meditation.

## Sapphire

Alas this rock is not one massive sapphire, but many small sapphires in quartz with a little mica and other minerals, too. Had it been one sapphire with a weight of about 1,000ct, I (Philip) would probably happily retire! It's not, but it fits perfectly in my hand and has its own worth. I like rubbing and stroking the rock when I'm thinking about nothing in particular, or sometimes when I'm reading. It doesn't really give me a solution, but when I put it down, I know where I'm supposed to look for the answers to the question I didn't know I was asking. It connects me to my spirit guides and opens my mind to possibilities.

## Lapis Lazuli Pyramid

This is a carved pyramid and naturally reminds me of the Egyptian pyramids at Giza. They have both astrological and afterlife connections. The pyramid's shape, the strong solid base rising to the apex, represents the dead pharaoh's passage to eternal life among the stars; or the reverse view, suggesting the sun's rays shining down and illuminating the four corners of the earth. Perhaps it symbolizes a meeting of the two worlds of the living and the dead. For me (Philip), and many other people, the shape acts as a focus for meditation. I concentrate on the tip and slowly bring my mind down the side of the pyramid, allowing my focus to move within the structure until I feel lost in a different inner world. Lapis lazuli is a stone that boosts all psychic abilities and aids creative expression.

## Indian Chief

This stone is one of my favorites. When I (Lyn) first saw this metamorphosis crystal, I loved the way it became pinker as I held it and thought about working with it. At first I saw it as quite a "girly" stone. After picking up a few different pieces, I was drawn to this one because it seemed a little pinker than its neighbors. As soon as I had it in my hand, I was amazed by the perfect fit; it just slotted into the contours of my hand and fingers. "That's it," I thought, "I'll choose this piece." I examined it further, surprised by the feeling of powerful energy coming from it. Then I noticed the profile of an Indian chief practically glaring out at the edge of the stone, full headdress flying back from his head. Not just any Indian chief, but a very proud, stern, and wise-looking chief, staring moodily straight ahead. I could see at once this was no "girly" stone, and was not one to ask frivolous questions but to consult carefully in a very proper and respectful manner.

He is a very serious stone and I always think carefully before I work with him. He is a chief among chiefs and very much revered, by me and by others who have encountered him. Metamorphosis crystal brings about change quite quickly and sometimes very dramatically, so be careful what you ask for, is the warning here.

## Aqua Aura

A very beautiful addition to the collection of special stones, and practical too. I (Lyn) work with this a great deal for healing and just love the way, when I hold it, the four "fingers" of crystal points seem to reach out to heal the person being treated. I first encountered this particular one when I was in our shop and a lady staggered in, shaking and with blood on her hands and legs, clothes spattered with dirt. She explained, in a strangely matter of fact way, that she had been knocked over from behind by a car, which didn't stop. Luckily, it had been going slowly, so she wasn't hurt badly, but had fallen into the muddy gutter. I asked if she'd like to come and sit upstairs in one of our healing rooms for a while and she just nodded.

As I walked through the shop with her to go upstairs, I gathered up a couple of crystals to help and one, which surprised me at the time, was this aqua aura crystal. These were a new type of crystal to us then. Having learned never to question a crystal that wants to assist, I took it along. The lady sat shaking, quite unable to speak further. With her consent, I moved the aqua aura crystal over her arms and legs and around her solar plexus, at which point she finally burst into tears and released the shock that had frozen in her. Since that day, I have always employed this crystal to help whenever I suspect delayed shock is trapped in a client I am working with.

## AGATES

Agates are a kind of chalcedony and come in a variety of colors, each with its own special qualities, but all agates are protective and nurture natural talents and relationships. I have several favorites among my stones.

## Pink-banded Agate Tumble-stone

This is the first stone Philip ever gave to me and so is very precious. She never fails to make me feel extra feminine when I carry her with me, and I always keep her nearby. Pink-banded agate helps to bring out everyone's feminine side.

## Agate Slice

Another agate I (Lyn) love is a slice with markings that look like a lilac lake with trees on the far shore. Many agate slices have beautiful natural pictures on them. As I gaze at this wonderful scene, I feel myself being drawn into the unfathomable deep mystery of the lakes, or the enigmatic tangle of the white forest. I like to keep it near me for inspiration when I'm painting.

## Agate Teardrop

This captivating agate slice, which is shaped exactly like a large teardrop, has an icy center, and can have a sad feel to it at times. As soon as it is held up toward the sun, though, it is immediately transformed by the light, and can be seen as a delicate leaf. I (Lyn) keep it near a window to catch as much light as possible!

## Agate Bookends

We love this pair of bookends. They have an almost perfect eclipse pattern of sun and crescent moon over the two halves. In folklore, eclipses have been viewed as bad omens, because they bring darkness, but this is only temporary and the light returns. Eclipses are very powerful times to make lasting changes in your life and remove blocks stopping you from progressing on your path.

Agate can act as a shield, protecting you on your spiritual journey.

## Amethyst Sphere

I (Lyn) call this my classroom crystal because this sphere has done a lot of hard work over the years and has assisted in many of my classes and courses. She is my talking ball, the female counterpart of Philip's talking stick. Whenever I teach, she sits beside me on the teaching mat, radiating her lovely energy into the room. I often pick her up and hold her in my hands to draw inspiration while expounding on a point. She always helps out.

In the important role of talking ball, she is passed around the students and the person holding her has everyone's attention while he or she is speaking. The sphere has a couple of other subtle jobs here, too. Sometimes class members become shy and a bit tongue-tied when having to speak to a group. Holding the ball gives them something to focus on, and the positive energy emitted gives them the courage to talk. If someone is really too shy to speak, or actually has nothing to say at this time, he or she can simply pass the ball straight on to the next person without having to say anything at all. It is understood. I am always amazed by the heat in the ball by the time it returns to me—the energies picked up from each person and activated by the amethyst itself create a precious, unique moment. I close my eyes for a few seconds to identify with the energies— a great way of bonding the whole group together.

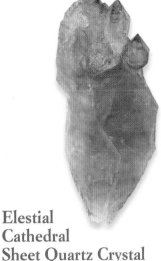

## QUARTZ

These are just three of my favorites; I (Lyn) do have many more!

## Tibetan Quartz

This one stays with me whenever I am writing. I love the chunky feel of him and the fact that he is in an "L" (for Lyn) shape. Whenever I look into this piece, I always seem to see new things that I have missed before, reminding me that there are always new ways of doing or saying something.

## Smoky Quartz Sphere

My little smoky quartz sphere was quite a find a few years ago. It is doubly protective because it has within it a needle-sized black tourmaline crystal rod. Both smoky quartz and all forms of tourmaline have protective qualities. It is absolutely stunning and quite unusual. I like to keep it beside my bed to protect me when I sleep.

## Elestial Cathedral Sheet Quartz Crystal

This is a very grown-up name for what I like to call my fairy castle crystal! It's also smoky quartz, so has an element of protection. As I look into the fantastic castle, high up on its rock, it reminds me of two types of fable—the quest to achieve something worthwhile, no matter how high the obstacles, and the fairy princess being whisked away by the handsome prince. The castle is a protective fortress, and besides that, this crystal has the ability to make dreams come true.

## Chapter 3

# Rock Art

This chapter leads you into your own creativity. There is no need to be a great artist, you just need the desire to put some color and your mark on a stone and to connect with it as you enhance and honor it. Just enjoy freeing up your inner abilities.

# ancient art

*The ancientness of stones and rocks gives them an essential and unique energy, which can be inspirational. Couple that with your own energy, essence, and intent and it can lead to the creation of a wonderful sacred stone for you to treasure and work with. Rock painting is a lovely way to spend a few hours and the whole process can be very therapeutic.*

Rock art has been around for thousands of years. Rocks and stones, so readily available, have lent their unique shapes and color to artists of all descriptions around the world throughout the ages. Egyptian wall paintings and Roman graffiti portraying the lifestyles of gods and humans are good examples, and going even further back in time, so are cave paintings and prehistoric carvings, etchings, and petroglyphs. We can only guess at the artists and their purposes. Prehistoric paintings often depict hunting scenes, which may have been used to teach young hunters necessary techniques, or as a way of recording the story of the hunt and to emphasize bravery in the chase.

The artists may simply have drawn and painted for the sake of it, or in response to the strong human urge to leave their mark. Stencils of hands are evident, as well as depictions of animals. Perhaps magicians painted the walls and then illuminated the paintings with fire to create fearsome effects during their sacred ceremonies and rituals. Or maybe then, as today, people just enjoyed leisure painting and decorating the walls of the places where they lived.

We all like to paint, although many people are not confident about their skill and may be shy of showing their efforts. This is a shame since much enjoyment is to be had from painting and it can be very therapeutic.

*rock art on stones*

LEFT A cave painting, possibly depicting a hunt.

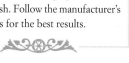

A great place for a stone with watery connections is at the bottom or edge of a shallow pond. Flowers or fish painted on the rocks around a pond can give a lovely show of color. Stones that are going to be kept outside or in water should be coated with polyurethane or yacht varnish. Follow the manufacturer's instructions for the best results.

Sitting holding a stone or a rock that you intend to paint can bring you very much into the moment. As you look around for inspiration and become more involved with the project, your worries and cares can drift away for a little while. Turn your rock in your hands, absorbing its energies, and you will find yourself entering more deeply into the possibilities. Look for natural imperfections that can magically turn into something to inspire or be incorporated into your painting. You may see a curled leaf, a mysterious eye, an exotic bird …

Another benefit is getting messy, drawing you back to your childhood where rules such as not getting dirty have no place or meaning. The creative instinct can overrule such grown-up laws.

## collecting your rocks

*Finding rocks, stones, and pebbles to paint can involve some beautiful walks. A small stone or two often finds its way into my pocket while I'm out walking the dog.*

The seashore, a shallow river, a hill or a mountain, the open fields, or the floor of a cave will all usually provide plenty of choice. Even woodlands can give up some interesting stones from time to time. The only problems are deciding which stones to pick up and carrying them home. Besides considering their weight, think about how you will want to display your rocks. Will they stay upright on their own or would they look better on a stand? Perhaps you want to mount them on a wall. If you are not sure what to choose, just pick up some random ones, but remember that smaller stones are harder to paint.

You won't have to go on many walks to build up a diverse collection. When you examine each one more closely at home, you'll be surprised at how much possibility you can see in what at first appeared to be a fairly plain rock. Don't be in too much of a hurry, let the rocks acclimatize and settle into their new environment, and look again in a few days.

## alternative sources

You can buy attractive stones in garden centers—and even paving slabs, if you want to paint something on a larger scale. Quarries are the places to find rocks in intriguing shapes. Builders' yards, and even car parks, can yield some goodies. Broken pieces in appealing shapes are especially good for painting landscapes on. Digging your flower beds may turn up an exciting specimen, possibly a half-finished flint tool, a shard of old pottery, or some other stone artefact. Hunting through a crystal or new-age store will produce unusual materials—just add imagination!

## selecting a rock for painting

*Some stones are perfect for completely covering in paint; others just need a touch or two to highlight what's already there. The very shape of a pebble can suggest the form of an animal or an object.*

Once you have carefully chosen a rock, possibly because something in it reminds you of an animal, a building, a bird, or a person, handle it gently. As your fingers trace the curves and indents in its natural structure, does it suddenly feel right in your hand? Are you entranced by its smoothness, coolness, energy, natural color, and texture? If so, put the stone aside. It's not an unusual occurrence, and it's no good returning to such a stone once this has happened. The stone's natural attributes are perfect without the paint, rather like a beautiful woman without make-up, and sometimes even a reproachful look is fleetingly apparent on the stone's surface if you dare draw a loaded brush near! Lovely rocks such as these need no embellishment from you and are best left alone for you to enjoy exactly as they are.

Other rocks almost beg to have their features enhanced and pictures revealed. Flat, smooth pebbles are easier to paint to start with, rather like a blank canvas waiting to be revealed as a painting of your choice. Later, you will find many different types of rock just lend themselves to your projects or suggest one you hadn't thought of before.

### finding the message

I (Lyn) have found many wonderful stones in various parts of the world. One of my favorites comes from a car park in Tucson, Arizona. It's a small flattish gray pebble— not very remarkable, but I was drawn to pick it up. Turning it over I saw that someone had drawn some squiggles on it, which I took to represent stormy waves below clouds moving in one direction, with one little breakaway cloud going in completely the opposite direction. I saw several possible messages in that: "It's okay to change direction when the going gets tough!" or "Don't lose your way!" but I settled on "Do your own thing!" All stones have messages, which we can access in different ways.

## the right time

The more time spent with stones, especially new additions, the more you become intuitive about them. Don't be deceived, though. I've (Lyn) kept rocks and stones for years, having picked them up randomly somewhere without strong reason or purpose. Once home, they appear quite boring or devoid of much interest so they end up in an odd corner somewhere. Then, one day, I look and there is a new face or energy that's so obvious—why didn't I see it before?

## magic of the stones

Other people may not be able to see what you can in a stone, even if you point it out to them. A friend may look at it this way and that and then pronounce, "No—can't see an eagle, but I *can* see an angel!" That's okay. You see what is important for you at the time. The stone has somehow shape-shifted for each person. The magic of the stones knows no bounds; it is held for endless time until released in whatever way is required.

## choosing themselves

When I think about painting something in particular, I go outside and walk among the stones I've collected until one keeps catching my eye. Rocks do that—"me, me, me!" you can almost hear them cry. I went to choose a rock for a cave painting and one flashed up almost immediately, a lovely, craggy, large rock with plenty of natural markings and a roughish texture. Perfect. I carried him off with great glee to give him a wash and brush up before we started work. I had also noticed a likely contender for a water-lily scene I wanted to do and decided to come back later for him. When I returned, another rock entirely was practically screaming at me: "Me! I can do it! I can do water lily! Choose me!" I looked at the previously earmarked stone, which kind of shrugged as I picked up Mr Eager. I must say we worked so well together, and I now have a gorgeous water-lily stone.

## naturally perfect

When Philip and I were on holiday in the South of France, I picked up some beautiful, round, smooth pebbles from a beach with the idea of bringing them home to paint with scenes from the area. I'd made some sketches on paper. At home, I washed them and put them outside to dry. However, when I brought out my paints and picked up one of the stones, it almost seemed to shudder. As I looked at its perfect shape and coloring and felt the smooth texture, I had to smile and put it down again, unpainted. In the summer, we would often absently pick one up and turn it over in our hands, simply enjoying its warm smoothness. The stones are useful paperweights, too, when a summer breeze whips up.

### friendship stones

I (Lyn) heard of a couple who used to have a "sorry" stone with a happy face on one side and a sad face on the other. If there had been an argument and one of the couple was ready to apologize and make up, that partner would move the stone from its resting place, where the happy face was uppermost, to its active place, turning it over to reveal the sad face. By moving the stone back to its resting place, the other person indicated that all was mended. I believe much hugging ensued! Another lovely idea is to paint two matching stones so that when you and your partner are apart, each can keep one of the pair.

For garden projects, acrylic paints that are made specially for outdoor work are available.

# projects

*When you think about painting a rock, don't worry. However it turns out, it's okay. We have kept our design suggestions simple (see pages 58–63) so that you can use them as a base from which to build up your ability. You could start by simply painting stones different colors. Shake them together in a bag and pick out your lucky color for the day.*

Painted rocks make great paperweights, bookends, and doorstops. Besides being decorative, they are practical and durable. You could use them for signs, such as "Beware of the Dog" or "Wipe Your Feet," and they could be made into short menus—so long as you are not planning to change things too often! Another useful message-on-a-stone is "Please do not disturb," which can be left outside a closed door or on the desk—invaluable for writers and artists and just about everyone at some stage! You could even have them as directional signs in the workplace—a simple arrow with the word "exit" underneath.

Another idea is to lay painted stones in the yard, or garden, to mark the way to a special place. And they

make wonderful gifts with angel messages painted on. You could personalize them with your own messages to friends or just paint their initials in flowing styles.

## deciding what to paint

You can paint just about anything onto a stone or a rock—for example, landscapes, animals, birds, trees, flowers, fruit. Totem animals and symbols, such as a star, moon, or sun, are a good idea. Fish, starfish, a lizard, or an insect are other suggestions.

Teaching stones have numbers or letters painted on individually, some with pictures to go with them. For example, three alphabet stones, **C-A-T**, would be matched with a stone that has a picture of a cat. These are very tactile and, used carefully, can enhance learning.

Keep notes of ideas for subjects or messages. Look at pictures, or use your imagination—something may just occur to you. Then look through your collection for a suitable stone. Whether you have an idea or prefer to be intuitive, meditation may help you to decide (see page 56). We all have spirit guides, although they are known by different names in different cultures, so start by asking for their help. Simply take a deep breath and imagine your spirit guide is with you, caring and protecting. You may picture your guide in your mind or feel the presence. Don't be concerned if you don't see or feel anything at first; your guide will come to you in time. Ask your spirit guide to help you paint your stones. Then continue with either of the following meditations. Keep some paper and a pencil nearby for drawing or writing down your ideas after you have meditated.

## choosing a subject

*If you have a rough idea of what you want to paint, sit in your painting space where you have set out everything, ready to begin. Make sure you are sitting comfortably and that you will not be disturbed. Ask your spirit guides for help.*

**1** Hold your chosen rock, stone, or pebble. Close your eyes and breathe slowly. Focus on your idea and breathe evenly. Count your breaths and stay focused, and watch until the image becomes very bright, detailed, and clear. When you have it firmly in your mind, slowly open your eyes, pick up your paper and pencil and draw it out. Thank your guides.

**2** If you would like your intuition to choose for you, while holding your stone, breathe, relax, and allow your mind to go completely blank. If you find this difficult, simply focus your attention on the inside of your forehead just above the bridge of your nose, or count your breaths slowly. It may take a little while or it may be that something comes to mind immediately; either is fine. As you continue to count, turning your stone in your hand, an image will begin to come into your mind. It may be a picture, a symbol, or a pattern, or it may be a word. It could be something you have never seen before. Once you have a definite image that you are happy with, take a deep breath, slowly open your eyes, and draw it out on your paper. Thank your guides.

## preparing to paint

For each project, decide where you want to do your painting. You may have a special space you can use, but if not, set up in the corner of a room, at the kitchen table, in the yard, or in the garden shed if it is raining, or out somewhere in nature—preferably somewhere quiet where you won't be disturbed and where you can stay in the moment with your stone. I read somewhere of one man who took all his stones and paints out into the desert and sat and meditated for a while and then just started painting one stone after another until he had exhausted his supply. When he had finished, he was quite bemused by what he had painted: many intuitive symbols, signs, and designs from his imagination. Some seemed to be divinely inspired.

If you are going to go out to paint, have a rucksack to put your materials in. Rocks can be heavy, so don't take too many at once unless you intend to drive somewhere you can unload your equipment easily.

## general check list

 These are the items you are always likely to need. With each sample design, we have included extras, specific to that particular project, and details of paints and paint brushes. (See pages 58–63.)

Large cloth or piece of paper

Plastic apron and rubber gloves

Paper towels and wipes

Jars of clean water

A palette

Spare plastic trays

Sketching paper and pencils

Tracing paper and removable tape

Two pastel pencils, or chalks, one
     light, one dark color

Plastic wrap

Hairdryer (optional)

Wherever you are, before you start painting it's a good idea to set out your materials. Lay out a large piece of paper or cloth to work on, to protect the surface underneath it. Wear old clothes, or a plastic apron. Some thin rubber gloves are useful as painting stones can be a very messy business. You will also need some paper towels and wet wipes to keep brushes clean and wipe up any spills.

I like to have three jars of clean water handy, to save having to fetch fresh water in the middle of the project. Plastic supermarket trays are fine instead of a palette for quick, small projects. You can throw them away afterward. Paper plates can be useful, but if you are outside, be careful they do not blow away. Use one of your pebbles to anchor them. For larger projects that are likely to take a couple of days, commercial palettes are available, which keep paints from drying out.

You'll need some sketching paper and a pencil for planning a design, and unless you are going to draw directly onto the stone, tracing paper and removable tape to hold it down. Also bring two soft pastel pencils, one in a light and one in a dark color for outlining your design onto the stone prior to painting, or a piece of chalk. If you are out and about, don't forget to add to your rucksack a pencil sharpener and a closed jar or two of water.

 If you want to paint your entire stone one color, or graduate it in stripes, the easiest way is to paint one side down as far as you can, leave it to dry completely, then turn it over and finish the other side.

Sponges used instead of brushes give a good and even cover. Synthetic household sponges are fine. Tear or cut them into small pieces, and into points for painting thin lines or dotting in an eye. Different textured sponges give interesting results. I have some very useful tapered sponge "brushes" with handles that I bought in America.

## brushes

These should suit the size of the stone you are painting. Choose a small, medium, or large-sized flat brush for covering larger areas, and a small, medium, or large round brush for all-purpose painting. You will also need an old brush or two for mixing paints and for dry scruffing paint onto the rock (see page 60.) A fine-liner brush is good for any detailed work and for lettering. Alternatively, you could use a fine permanent marker for this.

 Leave the stone to dry thoroughly before adding any design—the good old supermarket plastic trays are very useful for this, and ridged ones are ideal.

## paints

Acrylic paints are the best to use. They dry quickly and the colors stay bright. Metallic bronze, silver, gold, and copper are good for highlighting tiny areas, and also for writing on the stones. Silver paint on an indigo background can be stunning. Pearlescent tinting medium is also lovely to add a hint of shimmer here and there, and a dash of sparkly nail polish gives an unusual effect. Watercolor paints are unsuitable for these projects.

## designs

*The following projects are simple and enjoyable to do. Just follow the instructions, treating them as guidelines. If your intuition takes over, it's okay to change a color or design to your own liking. As long as you are pleased with the result, it's not important if your stones turn out differently from the illustrations. Gather the materials on the general checklist (see page 57.) Anything else needed is listed here. Color names can vary with different paint manufacturers, so choose the colors that appeal to you.*

## smooth pebble paperweight

**Extras you will need:**
Fairly large, flattish washed pebble
Medium flat brush or piece of sponge
Small round brush
Old brush for mixing
Paints: Indigo blue, violet, light blue, turquoise, white, a darkish green; pearlescent tinting medium

1 Squeeze some indigo and a touch of violet paint onto your palette and mix together using an old brush. Rinse the brush. Use your flat brush or piece of sponge to cover one side of the stone with paint. Set it aside to dry—you can speed up the process with a hairdryer. Cover your palette with plastic wrap to prevent the paint from hardening. Wash your brush or sponge thoroughly between each step.

2 Once dry, turn the stone over and cover this side with the same paint. Set aside to dry.

3 When the stone is completely dry, decide which way up it is to be. Check for markings and that it "sits" well without rolling about. Squeeze violet, light blue, and turquoise paint onto your palette. Using the round brush, lightly paint random streaks in each color to represent water. Wash and dry the brush each time before changing color. Leave to dry.

4 Take the light colored pastel pencil or piece of chalk and roughly mark out where you would like your water lilies to be. Little groups of three are pleasing. Make them of various sizes and don't be tempted to do too many. Simply dampen a finger or piece of clean sponge to wipe off any mistakes. Then, squeeze some white paint onto your palette and, using the point of your dry round brush, make quick little semicircles over your pencil marks. Directly above the semicircles, dot in some white for the flowers, making sure they are not regimental but of different sizes and strengths. Leave to dry.

5 With the very tip of your dry round brush, pick up a tiny spot of violet paint and dot it into the center of most of the white flowers. Rinse your brush. Next, squeeze a little of the green paint onto your palette. Dip your brush into clean water and shake off the excess. Pick up some green paint and lightly paint a shadow under the semicircles of white. Don't worry if you touch onto the white lilies here and there—it just adds to the effect. The dampness of your brush will allow the shadows to be of different strengths, lightening and darkening to enhance the watery effect. Leave to dry.

6 When all is dry, squeeze a little pearlescent tinting medium onto your palette, pick up a tiny amount on a clean, dry round brush and lightly dot or stroke over one or two areas to highlight a flower, or give the water a shimmer. Don't overdo this. Leave to dry completely. You now have your water-lily stone to use as a paperweight, or perhaps place in your pond.

## cave painting

*You may like to spend some time meditating or getting in touch with your spirit guides for inspiration before beginning this project. (See page 55.)*

Choose any sized rock so long as it is rough in texture, an uneven shape, and if possible, has some natural markings. (The one in the illustration is hand-sized.) Ideally, your rock should be either chunky and freestanding (like the one shown) or flat with uneven edges to represent the wall of a cave. Study it carefully and choose what you want to paint on it, and where on the rock you want to site the picture or symbol. Every rock is different in texture, coloring, and shape and you will need to choose something that will partly follow its natural lines. By closing your eyes and handling the rock, you may be able to "feel" the image that wants to be brought to life in your painting. Otherwise, look at the photograph here for ideas, or Google "cave paintings," which will produce some good images of animals and symbols to guide you.

### Extras you will need:
Your chosen rock, washed and thoroughly dried
A medium flat brush and some pieces of sponge
A small round brush
A fine-liner brush, or fine permanent markers, one
   red and one black
An old brush

### Paints:
Black, and a couple of earthy colors—choose from burnt umber, raw umber, burnt sienna, raw sienna, or any browns that you may have—some yellow ochre, a tiny amount of ultramarine blue, and a fairly bright red. Scraps of paper to test your mixes on

1 Squeeze a little of each of your paints separately onto your palette. Leave the red to one side to use later. Experiment with mixing the browns and the earthy colors—a dab of just two of them each time—to produce some good, cave-like shades, the duller and muddier the better. Add a touch of yellow ochre and test on a scrap of paper. When you are satisfied with two or three different shades, take your old brush, keep it dry and pick up some of your first chosen mix. Press down so the bristles splay and drag roughly in different directions over the rock, alternating with a scrubbing action—hence the old brush! This is known as scruffing. Don't load the brush too full with paint. You are not aiming to cover the whole rock by any means—the rock's own surface will serve as color, too. Dip your brush into each of the plain browns in turn and apply to the rock. Do the same with each of the mixes, the yellow ochre, and the ultramarine blue. Scruff a couple of colors here and there. Wipe your brush on a piece of paper towel

to remove the excess each time. Do not wash the brush between picking up the colors because it needs to remain dry to give the right effect, and the colors blend naturally on the brush. Work quickly as the paint dries fast. You have now prepared your "canvas". Leave it for a while to dry, and wash your brush thoroughly.

**2** With the pastel pencil, or chalk, draw your main outline—in this case the bison—onto the rock. Tracing would probably be difficult owing to the lumpy texture of your rock, so freehand is best; and with a cave painting, the more irregular the figure the better. Once you are satisfied with your outline, take your round brush or black permanent marker and paint over it, adding any details, such as eyes, with your fine liner brush or marker. Don't worry if your brush misses here and there—it all adds to the atmosphere of the cave drawing. Do this fairly quickly and do not try to go back to perfect the outline. Wash and carefully dry the brushes.

**3** The next stage is to paint on one or two simple geometric signs and symbols, usually a combination of straight or curved lines and dots. You may like to spend a little time meditating or contacting your spirit guides for inspiration about the designs, or Google "cave paintings," but for the purposes of this exercise, you could just copy those shown opposite. Don't overdo the number of symbols; one or two, carefully placed, will have more impact than if they are crowded on.

When you are ready, use the pastel pencil or chalk to mark the symbols on your rock, looking for intriguing locations to place them for the best effect. Take your clean, dry, fine-liner brush, or use the edge of your flat brush, and pick up some of the red paint already on your palette. Add a touch of brown to dull it a little if it is very bright. Again, experiment on paper first. If you are using a marker pen, test it first on the base of your rock to see if it is suitable.

For the first sign, draw a thin, short line either straight or following the curve of your rock. Above it, place three small red dots, using the tip of your round brush. Next, using your fine-liner brush or red marker, draw a slightly shorter line above two of the dots.

Choose another place for the second symbol, and simply dot five spots of red forming a circle. The third symbol is made up of a vertical line with four horizontal lines either side, rather like pairs of stick-people arms, very slightly curving downward and reducing in size as they get lower. Start them from about a third of the way down the vertical line, ending at the bottom, with what looks like two little legs.

And that's it! You have your own cave painting. All that's left to do is to sign it and date it somewhere on the bottom.

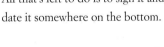

## paint a landscape

*For this project we have chosen an Arizona landscape at sunset. Select a rock that is shaped to suit the landscape you have chosen to paint, or pick up a flattish rock and study it until an idea presents itself to you.*

**Extras you will need:**

A flattish rock, or a piece of slate

Several pieces of sponge and a tray of water to rinse
    them out

A flat brush

A round brush

A fine-liner brush or fine black marker pen

An old brush

**Paints:**

Black, red, orange, yellow, and quinacridone magenta

1 On a piece of paper, draw the outline shape of your rock and adapt the landscape to suit it. Practice until you are happy with it, and then lightly copy it onto the rock with the pastel pencil or chalk.

2 Squeeze onto your palette some of the red, orange, yellow, black, and a little quinacridone magenta paint. Dip a piece of sponge into the orange paint, and wipe it across your rock from the top in horizontal movements down to the peak of the mountains. Don't worry about it being even. Next, on the same piece of sponge with the residue orange on it, pick up some red and lightly streak it over the orange. Add a little more orange and wipe across underneath the red; then use a little yellow and

streak the sponge across under the orange. Next, pick up some more red, again on the used sponge, and continue wiping in horizontal passes down to the top of the mountains. Leave to dry. Rinse your sponge to prevent it hardening.

Pick up a little more yellow on the tip of a clean brush or point of clean sponge, and make a couple of random thin streaks across the orange area. With a clean brush or tip of sponge, add a little of the magenta and streak a couple of random fine lines through the red colors at the top and bottom of the sunset. Wash brushes and sponge. Leave to dry.

3 With the flat brush, pick up some black paint and fill in the mountains. Still with black, using the round brush, paint in the trunk and larger branches of the tree. Using the point of your round brush, the fine-liner brush, or marker pen, add in the smaller branches. Leave to dry and wash out your brushes.

4 With the old brush, pick up some black paint and scruff among the branches to represent the leaves. Don't overdo it. You can also use the tip of the round brush or liner for detailing the leaves. That's it! Don't fiddle, you're done!

## your sacred stone

*This can be anything you want it to be—a traditional sacred picture, a symbol, some script, a prayer, or something of your own design, perhaps incorporating several meaningful aspects of your life.*

*For this example, we have chosen the Heart-line Bear. This character first appears as a helper in creation stories in Native American tradition, representing different things to different tribes, generally strength, leadership, and protection. He is a healer. The heart line is the path the breath takes; it can be compared to the life-force energy of the animal spirit. The arrow depicts direction of movement or force.*

**Extras you will need:**
A smallish, flat round pebble
A flat brush or sponge
A small round brush
A fine-liner brush
A fine marker pen
A drawing or tracing of a Heart-line Bear
**Paints:**
Turquoise and black

1 Squeeze some turquoise and some black paint onto your palette. Paint your stone all over with the turquoise paint, using the flat brush or sponge, leaving it to dry between painting the top side and the under side.

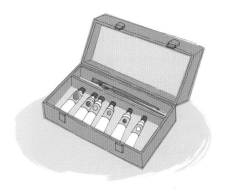

2 Make a tracing of the Heart-line Bear.

3 When your painted stone is completely dry, transfer the tracing onto it, holding the tracing paper in place with some removable tape. Be careful it doesn't peel up any of the base color when you remove it. Alternatively, draw the bear freehand onto your pebble with the pastel pencil or chalk.

4 With either the fine marker pen or fine-liner brush, carefully go over the outline of the bear on your pebble, and also the outlines of the pattern markings on the bear's side. Next, again carefully, fill in the bear with black paint, using a small round brush or the fine-liner brush, leaving the patterns in turquoise. That's all there is to do! Leave to dry and wash out your brushes and sponge.

## Chapter 4

# Working with your Sacred Stones

In this chapter we explore the possibilities that are created when you work with sacred stones, both large and small. Add them around your home, communicate with them, sense their energy, and follow their guidance.

# practical exercises with sacred stones

*There are many things you can do with your stones and crystals, once you have them, and always remember that your collection isn't fixed. You can, and most certainly will, add to it and take from it as time goes by. You will find that, just like human friends, some of your crystal companions will stay with you for a lifetime while others will come and go as they are needed.*

To help you understand your stones and experience for yourself their mysterious and magical powers, try the exercises described in this chapter. This will help you to enjoy working with your growing stone collection, enabling you to experience more fully the capacity your stones and crystals have to enhance your life.

*pyrite*

## crystals around your home

*Firstly, let's look at your home. There is nowhere that crystals cannot be placed to help make your home, and those occupying it, feel more comfortable and balanced, more relaxed and agreeable. So ask some of your lovely crystals to begin working on your behalf.*

Armed with a notebook and a pen, go for a wander around the house. Write down the name of the room as a heading and list the activities and restful occupations that might take place there. Then, ask yourself how this could be improved. Perhaps you are in the kitchen right now and your child is at the table, trying to do his or her homework. If there really is nowhere else for him or her to go, and other members of the family tend to gravitate there,

too, make a note to place some pyrite on the table, to create a barrier between the worker and the general hubbub of whatever else is going on in the kitchen—someone preparing dinner, for example, opening and shutting cupboards, and chopping vegetables; or maybe the washing machine is on full spin. Pyrite is wonderful at creating such a barrier, and also works extremely well placed on a window sill to prevent outside distractions.

There could be a job for some more pyrite in your home's general living area, or for some crystals, such as smoky quartz, to protect personal space. If this is a busy room, used for hobbies and lively activities, some amethyst to help prevent the energies depleting might be helpful. Amethyst also boosts general health and well-being.

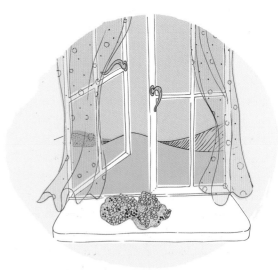

Now you have some ideas, carry on wandering around your home, noting down the areas that may *smoky quartz* need some crystal help and light. Find out from a reliable crystal book what would be good to have in particular rooms and corners of rooms, on desks, under beds, on bookcases, in bathrooms. You have a wide scope to choose from, so enjoy yourself! There are no rules to follow here, just your own intuition and preferences. If you are drawn to a crystal as you are going around the house, and feel it would suit somewhere specific, trust yourself and put it there. You can always check your intuition with your dowsing crystal pendulum later. (See page 16.)

You might like to sit in a room, close your eyes, and see how that room feels. What does it lack? Warmth, peace, vitality? Place a few carefully chosen crystals in the same room, go away and come back later to see if you can sense any changes. Sit down in the same spot as before, again with your eyes closed. What do you notice? Adjust your crystals, either by moving them to different places in the room or removing one or all of them completely and replacing with others.

It's good to take time over this. If you want some crystals in the bathroom, choose some to have with you while you take a long, luxurious soak in the bath or a refreshing shower. Then see how you feel about your crystal choices.

The key is to pick an occasion when you are not in a hurry and can spend time sensing and feeling the ambience where your crystals are. Keep making notes as you go and keep a record of what you have put where. After a while, if you sense that one room doesn't feel quite right, have a look at what you wrote originally and at the crystals themselves. Do the notes that you made still apply? Are the crystals looking bright and happy? Make any adjustments needed, and cleanse your crystals regularly (see page 118).

Remember that a garden is part of your home, too, so spend some time outside with your notebook, finding out what crystals might be valuable to place there. You could try the same exercise at your place of work to create a more harmonious setting for yourself.

# messages from your stones

*Stones have a way of communicating in an unseen dimension. Sometimes their physical attributes guide you to the answer, but often the link is subtle. Something spiritual that you can't quite identify points you in the right direction.*

It is as if the Stone People (see page 86) have their own language and you are learning it. Sometimes you catch a word and understand the message; sometimes you grasp the meaning of a whole speech, with all its nuances and inflections.

Stones have been revered for their prophetic qualities since Stone Age times and, since then, have been cast, picked, dowsed, and simply observed. You can speak to—and, more importantly, listen to—stones in a number of ways. Meditation, divination, and dowsing are three of the most widely used.

## crystal meditation

Meditation is an art as ancient as mankind; for example, the idea of contemplating a beautiful sunrise or sunset, being awed at the wonder of nature or the simple attraction to a pebble or crystal. Meditating allows us to find more of ourselves and experience the world around us to a greater extent. This exercise is designed to help you start your meditation practice—to focus on a specific crystal, stone, rock, or boulder and connect with it so you can discover more of your inner self and a deeper meaning to your stone. If you already meditate, try adding this exercise to your meditation routine.

---

### communication

Everything you do with your crystals and stones is about communication, whether you are talking to them, listening to them, or letting their color, shape, and energy affect you subconsciously on a psychological or physiological level.

---

*The size of your stone does not matter, but for the purposes of this exercise we are going to work with a small crystal that will fit in the palm of your hand. You can adapt the exercise for working with large standing stones and stone circles. (See page 14 for other suggestions.)*

1 You may already have your own sacred space, either permanent or temporary, but if not, prepare a special area for yourself. This can be as straightforward or as elaborate as you like. The basics are that you should sit comfortably, perhaps in a favorite armchair, turn off your phone, dim the lights, and, if you wish, light a candle and play some relaxing or mystical music.

2 Select a crystal that you feel drawn to. Hold it in your hand. Look at it and allow yourself to be aware of the stone. Notice the shape and texture, whether it's smooth or sharp, rounded or flat, natural or polished. See the color, close your eyes, and continue to see the color in your mind. Imagine the color diffusing into your hand.

3 Take a deep breath and imagine this color flowing into you. Take a few more deep breaths and imagine the color flowing through you and filling you with its light.

4 In your mind, ask any question for which you'd like an answer. It doesn't have to be deep and meaningful; it could be about the weather or what to wear that evening. As we've said before, each crystal or stone is unique; some will be interested in the deep and meaningful and others will be more concerned with day-to-day matters. In the same way, you wouldn't have the same depth of conversation with all of your friends and acquaintances.

5 Now just sit quietly and wait for a reaction. It may take a few minutes. You may hear an answer or just know it. You may see the answer in your inner vision. When you start, you are more likely to notice something in the stone, such as a significant change in temperature, either hotter or colder, or a feeling inside you that moves up or down the front of your body, or perhaps a shiver through your spine.

Sometimes you will know exactly what these sensations mean, while at other times the answers may not be so clear. The more you practice this meditation exercise with different crystals, the easier it will become and the clearer your understanding will be of the messages in each of your different stones.

## crystal divination

Crystal divination can be formal, as with the use of my crystal Tarot cards, or much less so. An example would be that you notice a crystal on your way out to work and pop it in your pocket. Later when you discover that you must do a presentation, you put your hand in your pocket, and find the crystal is kyanite, which helps with public speaking.

We've mentioned dowsing (see page 16), and crystals are popular pendulum weights. This is because their energy makes this ancient art even easier. In the healing sense, the dowsing crystal will also begin the healing process as it answers your questions.

### visionary voice

No matter how many times we perceive it, the ability of stones to predict the future is always amazing. One case sticks in my mind. A client was continually drawn to crystals associated with change. In her treatment I (Philip) dowsed eudialyte for her and gently suggested that emotional changes were on the horizon. Then she picked an Apache tear for herself, which hinted that perhaps she'd be releasing emotions or shedding tears because of this change. On her way out through my shop, she bought an ametrine butterfly. The ametrine's gold and purple colors implied a change from one situation to another, and the butterfly is the classical animalistic image of change—a wonderful new beginning as it emerges from its dull chrysalis.

At the door, just as she was about to leave, she turned back, saying there was something else she had felt drawn to on the way in and wanted to buy. It was a small specimen of crocoite crystal, which is associated with the really big changes in your life, such as divorce and moving house. It was so obvious that I told her she had big changes coming in her life very soon. When she came for her session the following week, she said that she was getting divorced and her husband had moved out. He wasn't arguing over anything—she would have the house. She had already decided to sell it and move to America, where she had family. Now that is what I would call *change*!

*eudialyte*

Some crystals work better for this exercise than others. Here are some readily available crystal suggestions. Amethyst, aventurine, aquamarine, carnelian, citrine, and red jasper all have energies that are quite different from each other, and easy to sense.

*amethyst*

*citrine*

*red jasper*

## sensing crystal energy

*We've already talked about sensing the energy of stones at sacred sites (see page 13). Now here's an exercise you can do at home, either by yourself or with a few friends, to help you test and encourage your ability to tune in to crystal energy.*

1 You will need a selection of crystals—choose ones of similar size so different types are not recognizable by size and shape. It is best to use tumble-polished stones for this exercise. They have the same intrinsic energy as natural crystals—perhaps less directed, but that is unimportant for this test.

2 Put your selected stones on a tray or into a box, bag, or some other container in front of you. Close your eyes, mix them up, and pick one stone.

3 Keeping your eyes closed, voice your feelings for the stone; speak into a recorder, or have a friend write as you speak. Start off with simple physical feelings. Does the stone weigh heavy or light? Is it warm or cool to the touch? Although polished, does it feel smooth all around its surface?

4 Then consider the effect the stone is having on you. Is it calming or energizing? Do you feel relaxed? Do you feel a little edgy or agitated? Are you feeling bright and alert or tired, even as if you could fall asleep?

5 After you have explored these feelings, see if you can notice the crystal's energy anywhere in your body other than in the hand holding the crystal. For example, can you sense anything in your arm? Or is there a sensation in your other hand? Is the feeling in your empty hand the opposite of what you are feeling in the hand that is holding the crystal, maybe one is warm and the other cool, or is it something completely different? Be aware of your body. Can you feel the crystal having any effect anywhere else in your body? Take your time over this. Pay particular attention to your seven major chakras (see page 119) and notice any feelings or sensations in these areas. Do you sense a color with this crystal? What are you thinking? Be conscious of the thoughts floating through your mind. Do they say anything about this crystal?

6 Repeat this process for each of the crystals in the container.

## programming crystals

By programming crystals we can increase both the speed of action and efficacy of the crystal. As we work with our crystals, they become naturally programmed. Simply doing the same thing with the same crystal over and over again helps to train both you and the crystal, and helps you to work better together. For example, you may have a crystal to take away pain. Quartz crystals do this very well (see page 47) and the first time you work with your crystal for analgesic relief it may take twenty or thirty minutes to have an effect—about the same time as a painkilling pill from the pharmacist. But as you repeat this exercise with the same quartz crystal, you will discover that the pain will dissipate quicker and quicker each time. In the end, you might not even need to have the crystal with you.

Intent is just as important. When you are choosing a crystal for a special task, think carefully about what is required of it, and see if you are drawn toward one in particular. You may have already narrowed the field from your own knowledge, or information gleaned about the type of crystal that might help. Once you have made your choice, you will need to cleanse (see page 118) and then program that crystal.

The massive stones at sacred sites are no different in this respect. They have been cleansed by the rain and programmed both by intent and by the repetition of ceremonies over many years before they fell into disuse. Sometimes, the specific material was so important that massive boulders were transported miles to their final position, such as the Preseli blue stones at Stonehenge. This is one reason why ancient sacred places still hold a magical feeling for many—it's imbued in the stones.

## understanding the messages

Don't be concerned if you and your friends appear to feel different things. We don't have a vocabulary for "energy," so tend to base our responses on experiences, describing our feelings by saying, "This feels like the time when…" All our lives are different, so it should not be altogether surprising that we express our feelings differently.

This is an exercise to confirm that you, like everyone else, are capable of sensing crystal energy. Take note of what you sense, but don't worry if it differs from the accepted norm for a specific crystal. For example, aventurine links to the heart chakra (see page 119), but you may have felt it in your throat chakra. This could suggest that you need to calm what you are saying to someone. If you're a singer, you may have strained your voice. Or it could be nothing of the sort; just that your mind is saying to you, "This reminds me of the time when I felt this sensation in my throat."

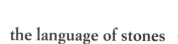

## the language of stones

All the time they speak to us. You hear almost as a whisper the voice of the pebbles you collected from the beach, or a stone you picked up at a stone circle, calling with ancient voice from the past. Your crystal collection may murmur gentle guidance but sometimes the stones shout at you to act. You see one shining with colorful rainbows inside and another sparkle as the light catches it, each one speaking in its own tongue. You've started to learn the language of the Stone People.

## directing your intent

*You can enhance or focus the power of crystals in many ways. Some involve mystical rituals and some are simple. This is one easy method to direct your intent into a crystal.*

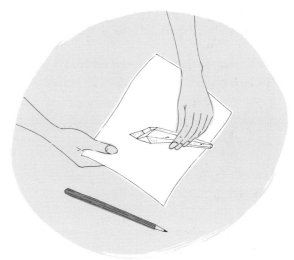

1 Choose a suitable crystal. Quartz crystals will hold any type of information, but sometimes you may prefer to choose a crystal that links directly with your purpose, such as moonstone if you are going to program a crystal to help you find a loving relationship. For this exercise, think about something simple that you would like a little help with—not too deep and meaningful to start. For example, I might choose to request help finding a parking space outside the supermarket on my next shopping trip. Then, just pick a small crystal, even the first one you see.

2 Take a moment to hold your crystal. Close your eyes and connect with it. See if you can feel a flow of energy between you and the stone. If after a little while you feel nothing at all, it could be that the crystal is remaining silent because it doesn't want to do this task, and you should choose another stone.

3 When you are happy with your chosen crystal and feel ready to continue, imagine your task being successfully completed. In this example, I'd picture myself driving into the parking space right outside the door of the supermarket. You might like to write down the outcome and place it under the crystal; or if your quest involves someone else, place that person's name or photograph beneath your stone.

4 When you've finished, thank the crystal for helping you and place it somewhere it won't be disturbed, or keep it with you and repeat this procedure daily until the event is manifested. You will become quicker and more efficient in this process as you practice, and your crystals will also speed up as they learn with you. Small things may happen instantly while more challenging requests may take several weeks or longer, but it's worth persevering.

## crystal grid

*You can energize an event or an idea, a concept or a goal, with a programmed crystal and a crystal grid. This takes you a step further, and can speed up and enhance the programming process. The technique can be particularly helpful with intangible concepts and ideas, or events that are distanced from you by time and space. It's also useful when you don't have the time to repeat the programming exercise above for several weeks.*

1 Choose six quartz crystal points. They represent the natural six sides of all quartz crystals. Place them pointing inward as if they were making up the six corners of a hexagon. You might like to draw a hexagon on a piece of paper and place the crystals in the six corners.

2 Now put the crystal you programmed earlier in the center of this crystal grid. Add a photograph or written request if either seem suitable. Some people like to secure the crystals in position. If you want to do this, use a putty-like pressure-sensitive adhesive or tape that will not damage the crystals.

### plant recovery

If one of your plants, either indoor or outdoor, is looking a little sad, you can help it with your stones. Use your intuition to choose some crystals, or look up suitable ones in your crystal book. You can also dowse some crystals for an ailing plant. Place your intent into the crystals by holding them for a moment or two and asking for their help in healing the plant, and then tuck them into the soil by the roots. It doesn't matter whether the plant is a flower, a herb, a shrub, or a tree. Leave it alone and return in a few days to observe the progress as your plant begins to recover.

3 Once you are happy with your arrangement, ask your crystals for the help you would like. In the previous example, that would be to find the parking space, and as this grid will be set up for as long as you care to leave it, to continue to find you great parking spaces!

The possibilities are endless and, although mysterious, the positive outcomes make life happier and easier.

Any size or type of animal can benefit from crystal energy. You could put some crystals around your birdcage or fish tank, for example, or place some calming crystals in corners of the stable of a highly strung horse—calcite might be a good choice in this case, to soothe its nerves. Crystals such as rose quartz or amethyst placed in the pens or sheds of farm animals could be of benefit to keep the animals relaxed and happy.

## animals included

*If you have animals, why not introduce them to your crystals? They may even like to choose some for themselves. Try this exercise with a cat or a dog.*

1 Lay out a varied selection of crystals. Choose sizes to suit the animal—not too big for it to pick them up in its mouth, but not so small that the stones could be swallowed.

2 Simply watch what your pet does and see which crystals it is drawn to. It may sniff each one but if you are patient, your pet will return to one or two in particular, eventually making its choice and claiming its favorite.

## night dream magic

Dreams can be wonderfully telling or just plain wonderful. Occasionally, though, dreams are not so nice, but by cleverly working with your crystals, you may find that you are able to influence the structure or fabric of your dreams. This may help you to obtain answers to questions that are bothering you, or you could just create fabulously mystical dreams. Who knows what the crystals will do when mixed with your psyche?

### what would you like to know?

The question you would like answered will influence your choice of crystals. You may want to know who your future partner in life will be, or whether you will get that new job; or perhaps you would like some inspiration for an art project, or creative writing. Don't expect the dreams to be exact; they are often symbolic. What they will do is work with your own subconscious to produce some clues for you. You may have to unravel these to make sense of them, and it may take several nights to complete the process.

# which stones to choose?

Celestite, lapis lazuli, and moldavite, to name a few, are all crystals that will help you to dream and to recall your dreams. Dream interpretation can be assisted by kyanite, larvakite, and smoky quartz. Metamorphosis quartz is always a good one to add to the team because it brings about change, and it has been known to do this in quite a fast and spectacular way.

By choosing your crystals with awareness, you will find that the specific energies of each one will work with you as you sleep, and because you are going to pre-program them, you will have the best chance of dreaming the dreams you want.

Once you have chosen your crystals, you could, as a further exercise, check up on the various properties they have. It may be that they have other assets that will create additional aspects to your dreams. You may have chosen one for something specific but it may also do something else, which would not be conducive to the result sought. Make sure you spend time choosing crystals carefully and being aware of the probabilities of the end result.

*Specific crystals placed under your pillow can help with special questions:*

MALACHITE: loves to help you sleep, so include this if you think you might have trouble sleeping.

RUBY: for help from the Akashic records.

DIAMOND: protects your aura while you sleep.

OBSIDIAN: connects you to your ancestors.

AJOITE: supports your connection to spirit.

AMETHYST: also supports your connection to spirit, and is protective.

FLUORITE: promotes teamwork and can help your crystals to work more efficiently together.

ROSE QUARTZ: for finding new friendships.

TURQUOISE: also for finding new friendships and protecting travelers.

## where should I put my crystals?

To an extent, this depends on the size of the stones
you have chosen. For instance, if you have decided
to move a large amethyst geode (cave) into the
bedroom, either the floor or a table anywhere in
the room will be fine. Its lovely energies will be
pervading the whole area around it all night and all
day. Your bedside table, or under the bed, are good
for medium or small-sized stones. You may even like
to take a few to bed with you, but choose carefully.
The smooth tumble stone variety are best, because
you don't want to wake up in the night with a jagged
crystal stuck into you. That might produce some very
uncomfortable dreams.

## tune in to your crystals

*Once you have chosen your crystal team, and are
ready for bed, put out the light and concentrate fully
on the stones. Keep a pen and paper by the bed ready
to make notes in the morning.*

1 Sit with the crystals individually and collectively,
and focus on the outcome you are hoping for. Close
your eyes and breathe deeply. Spend as much time as
you feel is necessary on this. It may be half an hour or
an hour; it may be just a few minutes.

2 Then lie down and sleep.

3 When you awaken, try to remember your dreams
before you open your eyes. Note down what you can
remember straightaway, before it fades. Later, read
your notes and see what you can interpret. Remember,
it may take a few dreams before you can make sense of
the message. It just takes a little practice.

## Chapter 5

# The Mystery of the Stones

Everyone loves a mystery and the stones contain plenty of those! Whether they look impressive and monumental or tiny and insignificant, each and every stone has a tale to tell. Some of their stone stories are legend, yet for others you may need to listen very carefully so their mysteries can slowly be unravelled, revealing a new secret to their fascinating library of knowledge.

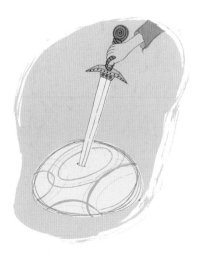

# special powers

*Stones of all sorts have an enduring link to the past, giving us a strong feeling of the energy they have drawn into themselves from their surroundings through all the different eras they have known. Sometimes the energy comes directly from the minerals that the stones contain, such as quartz, which is found in many types of stones, particularly those used for building sacred sites.*

OPPOSITE Mên-an-Tol, or Crick Stone, in Cornwall in the West of England has magical healing powers.

Crystals have been written about since before biblical times, from the days of ancient Greece, when Theophrastus acknowledged them, up to the modern day, when they are cited by scientists and healers. William Byrd, in his 16th-century musical elegy "Ye Sacred Muses" on the death of his colleague and sometime mentor, Thomas Tallis, referred to "crystal heav'ns above." James Rado and Gerome Ragni preferred "mystic crystal revelations" in the song "Aquarius" from their 20th-century

## ancient wisdom

In this classic tale, the sword referred to is Excalibur. The story relates how the boy King Arthur was accepted by the English nobility to lead them against all the invading hordes of the day. In the late 5th or maybe early 6th century, there was a dispute among the English aristocracy about who was the true heir to the recently deceased king, Uther Pendragon. Many claimed the title, but the nobility couldn't agree among themselves who rightfully should lead them. It was believed that the king was divinely appointed. Just prior to his death, Uther Pendragon had driven his sword, Excalibur, into a rock, saying that only his true and rightful heir would be able to remove it from the stone's clutches. The sword had been divinely created and presented to him by the great magician, Merlin. Many men, great warriors, some of noble birth some not, tried with all their strength to pull the magical sword from the rock, but all failed. Then along came young Arthur Pendragon and, with almost no effort, pulled out the sword. It was almost as if the stone had handed it to him, and so the legend of King Arthur was born.

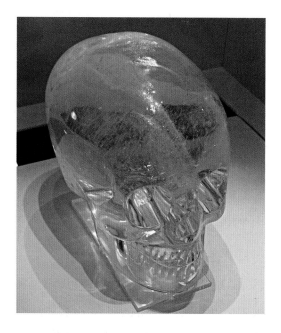

musical "Hair." Throughout the ages, their glories have been extolled, and the sacred, mysterious, wondrous world of crystals recorded in the music and literature of the day, so that the stories, tales, legends, and folklore surrounding them are legion.

# crystal skulls

*In an earlier time in South America, a strange and powerful band of wizards and magicians are said to have lived, possibly originating from an alien world, or maybe Atlantis. They were definitely not locally born, and they had fantastic powers and were adept healers. Eventually, they all died, and their bones were scattered. Thousands of years later, an explorer discovered a crystal skull.*

The skull was the size and shape of a large humanoid skull and was believed to be pre-Columbian Mesoamerican, although later tests brought this into doubt. Apparently, there are 13 of these crystal skulls, each of which has astonishing healing qualities. Many people who have been near them have reported feeling a power or a force field, and also experiencing healing and a feeling of wellness. One theory is that if ever all 13 crystal skulls come together, the whole planet will be healed of all its ills and wars will end.

# spirit of the stone

*Many stones were, and still are, considered to contain a spirit, mostly helpful, although some spirits can be badly behaved—hence the idea of lucky and unlucky stones.*

A stone may lie innocently along the wayside, not doing very much at all until someone comes along, picks it up, and slips it into his or her pocket. Now here's a chance for a spirit to enter the stone, to bring about just what this person needs or deserves, be it health, love, wealth, or even bad luck in the form of tripping up or losing something. It may be the ripening of karma, good or bad.

## opal

According to an ancient belief, the Storm God was so enraged at Rainbow ending his storm that he broke Rainbow into a thousand tiny pieces, which fell to Earth and became embedded in the rocks, creating Opal.

*pink opal*

To some, the gemstone opal is known as "the stone of thieves" because in the Middle Ages opals were reputed to cure eye problems—wrapped in a bay leaf, an opal would sharpen the sight of its owner and weaken the sight of opponents, thus bestowing the gift of invisibility. So it was named "Patronus Furum," the Patron of Thieves.

By the 14th century, opal had become a popular stone for jewelry throughout Europe. In 1348, Venice, Italy was devastated by earthquakes, tidal waves, and bubonic plague. Almost half the population died. Survivors noticed that opals would become brilliant when someone caught the plague but lose their luster as the sufferer neared death. This may seem magical, but has a relatively simple scientific explanation. Biochemical changes in the skin affect opals when they are worn next to it.

It is rumored in some circles that opal is an unlucky stone. We don't feel any type of crystal is unlucky but …

✳ The coaches in which Louis XIV of France traveled were named after gemstones, and Opal was known to be "unlucky." However, this was possibly because the driver was often inebriated and had many accidents.

✳ Napoleon gave a famous, stunning opal, "The Burning of Troy," to Josephine, who promptly lost it!

✳ During the latter part of the 19th century the stone called the "Grand Opal of Spain" is said to have brought disaster to the Spanish royal house. The story goes that Prince Alfonzo fell in love with the beautiful Countess de Castiglione. When he became Alfonzo XII, she thought she would become his queen. However, he married Princess Mercedes instead. Vowing revenge, she sent Alfonzo a magnificent opal set in a filigree ring of gold—a popular Spanish design of the day—as a wedding present. This gift was sent with the message "in memory of the old friendship." The new Queen Mercedes took a fancy to this stunning gem and asked her husband to grace her finger with it. A few months later she died of a mysterious illness. Alfonzo gave the ring to his grandmother, who passed away shortly afterward. The king next gave the ring to his sister, who was in turn carried off by the same mysterious illness. The king's sister-in-law had apparently always wanted the ring and she, too, breathed her last soon after receiving it. The king then wore it himself and in a few months the illness, which had taken so many of his family, ended his life, too. Then, new queen, Christina, put the ring on a chain around the neck of a statue of the Virgin of Alumdena, the patron saint of Madrid, and the curse on the royal family seemed to be lifted.

This story is in essence true. Cholera raged in Spain at this time and it has been estimated that, in all, half of the population died from the disease. A traditional quality of opals is that they protect against cholera, and so Alfonzo continued to pass this gem around his family to keep them safe. The Countess de Castiglione was able to reverse the opal's effect—by means not recorded—and so to "attract" cholera. This is another example of crystals "working," although not healing in this case.

## jet

From ancient civilizations right up to the present day, countless stones have been employed for protection and to help contact spirits in some way. They were often carried and worn as talismans or amulets. For example, jet, which in centuries past was known as black amber, was once acknowledged to give protection against many things. Its naturally dark color was thought to ward off the evil eye, and remove the effects of negative forces, such as witchcraft and curses from evil beings. It was also thought to chase away melancholy and unease, which may be another reason, besides its color, why jet was a popular choice in Victorian times for mourning brooches.

### in death

Stones have been called in to help with spells and magic of all kinds. Crystals have been found placed in ancient graves to bring protection to the deceased from evil spirits. In fact, stones are still placed on graves by people of many cultures. Certain stones, such as lapis lazuli, were more commonly called upon to exert their magic to assist the deceased to enter the next world without mishap. The ancient Egyptians often entombed a scarab made of lapis lazuli with the revered deceased person, believing it offered protection on their journey to the afterlife.

## jade

Regarded as a lucky stone, jade is highly valued throughout the world. In China, it is symbolic of love. A carved jade butterfly is a popular love token, often given at weddings. Amulets made of jade, often carved into the shapes of animals, are thought to protect the wearer against untimely death. In pre-Columbian America, the Maya wore jade amulets as protection against kidney problems. Strangely, Spaniards arriving in the New World were also wearing them for the very same reason.

## turquoise

Another lucky stone, turquoise brings protection and healing to the wearer. It was revered by the ancient Egyptians, found in tombs, and also placed to guard their burial grounds. Turquoise is much favored by Native Americans as a traveling stone. Native Americans also work with turquoise to connect with the sky spirit, Father Sky, to ask him to bring rain to increase crop yields and so prosperity. Turquoise is said to detect poisons or sickness by changing color from dark to light.

*quartz cluster*

## quartz crystal

In various cultures, quartz crystal is reputed to be the "most powerful crystal," the "grandfather crystal," and "Chief of the Stone People." The ancient Greeks believed that crystals were frozen light from heaven, or holy ice. The word crystal is derived from the Greek *crystallos*, which means ice. Onomacritus (c. 530–480 BCE), a Greek compiler of oracles, said, "Who goes into the temple with this [quartz crystal] in his hand may be quite sure of having his prayer granted, as the gods cannot withstand its power."

### changing color

Stones are shrouded in many mysteries, one of them being their ability to change color, which many of them do subtly or, in a few cases, quite dramatically. There are several reasons for this. One is because they are "overworked and underpaid" and have lost their luster as they need cleansing (see page 118); or they may be suffering from lack of attention, and be a little dull for this reason. On the plus side, very often they change color and brighten because they have been activated to do something. This may be totally due to someone's intent, or programming, or because the crystal has been activated in some other way. For example, metamorphosis stone exhibits a subtle change in color from a milky white to a pale pink. The clue is in the stone's name—it brings about a change in the person working with it, and the color change is a sure sign that the crystal is working. Clear quartz is also prone to showing definite changes, such as beautiful rainbows within the crystal and a general sharpening of its clarity.

## agate for bravery

Biblical tradition associates agate with the lion. A hair plucked from a lion's mane was said to be a source of courage, but luckily for many a brave man in need of such courage, agate was considered a suitable substitute!

# the Bible

*Among the 200 mentions of crystals in the Bible is the story of the Ten Commandments, which were written on "two tablets of stone" by the Hebrew prophet Moses. It is reported that "God showed him [Moses] a quarry of sapphire" from which he carved the second pair of tablets for the Ten Commandments, after he destroyed God's original work when he saw the Golden Calf (the full story is in the Old Testament and Chumash.)*

Moses was allowed to keep the chippings of sapphire from the quarry, the sale of which made him incredibly wealthy. "Sapphire" may have been a general term used in the ancient world for blue stones, and often referred to lapis lazuli, which was more freely available and much easier to carve. If God is omnipotent, then carving sapphire would have been no problem, but if the commandments were dictated by Him and physically carved by Moses, then, around 5,000 years ago, Moses would have carved them in lapis lazuli.

# stone people

*Native people around the globe have traditions concerning crystals, stones, rocks, and minerals. Native Americans call them the Stone People. Each stone has a spirit within, an* inyan, *which is a child of Mother Earth. These are the oldest and wisest beings on Earth. Every person has a special stone, a* watai, *which forms a bond with them and imparts wisdom and healing. These are Lakota words but all native peoples have their own words to describe these beliefs.*

An old Cherokee legend suggests that the animals became unhappy with man's destruction of the environment, so each animal brought a disease into the world. But the Plant Tribe and the Stone People thought more kindly of man and brought remedies for the animals' illnesses. Each plant chose a healing force to embed within its growing structure, but subtly, so that man would have to honor and be aware of the plant to gain its healing properties. One plant in particular spoke out. This was Tobacco, the chief of the plants. He said, "I will be the sacred herb. I will not cure any specific disease, but I will help people return to the sacred way of life, provided I am smoked or offered with prayers and ceremony. But if I am misused, if I am merely smoked for pleasure, I will cause the worst disease of all."

The Stone People agreed that, likewise, each mineral would have a spiritual power, a subtle vibration that could be used to regain perfect health. Ruby, worn as an amulet, would heal the heart; Emerald would heal the liver and eyes, and so on. The chief of the mineral tribe, Quartz Crystal, was clear, like the light of creation itself. Quartz put his arms around his brother Tobacco and said, "I will be the sacred mineral. I will heal the mind. I will help human beings see the origin of disease. I will help to bring wisdom and clarity in dreams. And I will record their spiritual history, including our meeting today, so that in the future, if humans gaze into me, they may see their origin and the way of harmony." And so it is today.

*ruby*

# holey stones

*Stones with natural holes that have been created by the process of erosion caused by water or wind have been revered since time immemorial, whether the stones are pocket sized or big enough to climb through. Holey stones are also known as Odin stones, after the Norse god who transformed himself into a snake to crawl through a hole in a stone in order to steal the sacred drink, or "mead," that inspired poetry.*

Another name is fairy stones. It is said that, with practice, when you look through the hole, you can see the faerie folk. This is probably an old legend to explain second sight or clairvoyance. They have also been called hag or witch's stones and many other colloquial names.

The larger stones are reputed to heal many ailments when you pass through the hole. The Mên-an-Tol, or Crick Stone, in Cornwall in the southwest of England, had a reputation for healing rickets in children, and for giving the gift of pregnancy when a woman passes through the hole seven times backward, at the full moon.

Holey stones do boost your powers of perception and intuition, and are helpful aids to meditation. In crystal healing, they can help with eye problems. Many people still work with holey stones today. Smaller stones can be carried or worn round the neck to protect you from harm on all levels—physical, emotional, mental, and spiritual. They are often hung in doorways or by windows to afford protection to a home or a business, and over a cot, a bed, or a pet's bed to keep the sleepers safe and ward off nightmares. Having a holey stone with you brings good luck. In rituals, they can represent the veil between the earth plane and spirit world.

## stones alive—the legend lives on

These legends and tales of old are added to every day from our own experiences. It's not just the stories from ages past, but the experiences from yesterday, today, and tomorrow that contribute to our ever-growing library of knowledge and the ongoing mystery of stones.

# sometimes the simplest of things

*The reason for being drawn to place a certain crystal in a specific location can sometimes be a mystery. For example, it may be that you absent-mindedly put down a crystal you were holding or working with in order to answer the phone and forgot to pick it up again. Then you are interested to note that the crystal in question is one of communication, such as blue lace agate, and you had an argument on the phone with your sister. Later, when you find the crystal again, next to the phone, it inspires you to call your sister to make amends.*

*blue lace agate*

Maybe you dropped a crystal by accident, a carnelian for example, and someone with the early symptoms of a cold spots it, picks it up, and slips it in their pocket, possibly with the intention of returning it to you if they know it's yours, or on a "finders keepers" basis. The energies of the carnelian may assist in boosting that person's well-being sufficiently to avoid the effects of the cold.

Sometimes just holding a stone and stroking it can release enough of its particular energies to calm or energize—whatever is needed at the time. All stones are very good at doing either or both.

## power bracelets

Buddha bracelets are made up of 21 beads, and used to keep track of the rhythm while chanting or meditating. They came to worldwide attention when the Dalai Lama wore them. Then celebrities, such as Robbie Williams, Richard Gere, and Madonna, took to wearing them, too, indicating their belief in the mystical powers of the gemstones from which the bracelets were made, and it became fashionable to wear them stacked up the arm. Power bracelets are made in many different crystals, bringing various powers to the wearer.

*carnelian*

## increasing power

*I (Lyn) feel I know some of the stones at various sacred sites as well as I have come to know each stone in my own collections at home, and like my crystals, they are individual. The mysteries locked into each of the stones are potent, but the extended powers of the group are even more effective. We all at some time feel that the more we have of something, the more power there is within it, and maybe that's what wealth really is all about; but in crystals and stones, it is infinitely more. Their potency increases more than by the multiplication of their number. It is a mystery. Try it out for yourself.*

**1** Sit holding just one crystal; notice how that feels. Meditate with it and let your mind fly free. Do you feel it?

**2** Collect a number of your crystals. Meditate with each one, noticing how they feel, all the time monitoring your inner experience.

**3** After that, put some crystals in a circle. Sit inside it. Observe how much more powerful the feelings are now as you close your eyes and allow the crystal energies to reach you. What are the stones revealing about you now?

### traveling stones

Some stones like to travel, moving from country to country in luggage or someone's pocket. A stone from Afghanistan may easily end up in Liverpool. Take, for example, Hertfordshire Pudding Stone, which is found only in Hertfordshire, England, having been pushed south during the last Ice Age and left behind as the ice retreated. It is a bane for farmers, ruining their ploughs. One such farmer was only too glad for us to remove the stones from his fields. We sent them to China to be cut and polished. The Chinese company sent most of them back, keeping some for themselves, and we sold them to a wholesaler in the north of England, who sells them all over the UK and continues to export them throughout the world.

## students' experiences

✵ During their second class, a group of students was asked what they had noticed about their crystals during the previous week. One woman said that for her it had been a "friendship" she'd struck up with a quartz crystal. As she put it, "It was a smoky quartz, which appeared to be almost talking to me, and seemed to balance and calm me almost immediately."

✵ After the students had been dowsing crystals for each other, one of them remarked: "The fact that these crystals were chosen for me at this stage of my life by someone who knows absolutely nothing about me, I find just astounding. These crystals confirm the words creativity, clarity, and communication all spelling out the changes I need to make to do the things I want to do now— clear the past completely and permanently, and learn to sculpt. I also want to overcome my shyness in speaking in front of an audience. In fact, some of these things are already beginning to manifest."

✵ When the students were dowsing each other to see if they could locate any issues residing inside their partner, it was wonderful to see the absolute amazement on their faces, not only at their new-found ability to work with a pendulum, but also at each new discovery of an area where a problem might be lurking. "Like magic!" and "How could you know that?" were among the comments. The stones really do love to work with students, showing how their energies can feel, and sometimes, well, just showing off!

### face the truth

One student mentioned that the set of crystals she had to work with made her feel extremely uncomfortable, but added ruefully that when she looked them up, she had to admit they were all pointing at things she usually spent most of her life avoiding. The stones always know the truth about us even when we don't want to own up to it.

✵ Some students mentioned that they were surprised to feel such differences between the energies of the crystals: some felt tingly and fizzy, others icy cold or very hot. They were also surprised by how a stone could create a feeling, such as a tingling sensation in the area of the chest, which could signify the need for that crystal's particular energy in that place at that time. The students' observations and interpretations confirmed to them that these crystal energies and mysteries were genuine.

✵ One student remarked that one of her partners in the class had chosen tiny stones for her, which she felt were a little insignificant and almost insulting—little did she know! Next time, she reported back that, when she had worked with them later that night, some very profound and life-changing revelations had come to her. Checking in her crystal book had confirmed her interpretations.

# Lemurian seed crystals

*A few years ago, Lyn and I were on our annual visit to the Tucson Gem and Mineral Show in Arizona, USA, when we happened upon a display of dazzling crystals in the sunshine. They were incredible because although they were definitely not the prettiest crystals on show, they were screaming for attention.*

Although they were quartz, they didn't quite look like any quartz crystals we'd seen before—and that's a multitude! As we browsed through them, at least two different energies became apparent—a group pull, as if they were all part of one entity, and the individual attraction of each stone. Some were almost jumping up and down and dancing on the tables, such were the vibrations coming from them. Others were just there, bright, brilliant, beautiful, but to be looked at like a painting in a gallery and not to be taken home like a friend. And then there were a few that really didn't want to know us. Each one of these would suddenly go dull in the sunlight as we focused on it, as if it was saying, "I don't want you," and hiding so it wouldn't be seen.

Just then the owner appeared as if out of thin air, although I think he'd been there all the time, watching and knowing, but it was just then that we noticed him. He explained that these were "Russian Lemurian crystals" and they were new. Now it was obvious to

us that they weren't "new"; they had to be at least 200 million years old! Over a bottle of mineral water he clarified the statement. They were a new find, a pocket of crystals, discovered the day after the 9/11 attack.

According to legend, the Lemurian civilization, which pre-dates Atlantis by 100,000 years, had been about to end in catastrophe. This was foreseen by their priests and they programmed quartz crystals with the knowledge of their society, and seeded them in a cave, sealing them in so they would be protected until the time was "right" for them to be rediscovered. The owner believed that these crystals would bring massive changes into the world, and that each one already knew who it wanted to work with and how to get to them, wherever they were. His role was to help them on their way.

## bizarre happenings!

I noticed Lyn had disappeared, but must admit I was more focused on these "new" crystals. I started selecting crystals, or were they picking me? As I was choosing, people's names and faces came to mind—customers in the shop, clients, friends. Occasionally, I knew I had to take a crystal, although it wasn't for me and I didn't know who it was for, but I knew that I would get it to the right person. That was bizarre—selecting a crystal specifically for someone I'd never met and had no logical reason to suppose I ever would meet. One crystal I remember said to me that it wanted to fly, and as we were returning home to the UK in three days' time, it was obvious it had to come with us.

Lyn reappeared looking slightly different—but I couldn't quite put my finger on how—and energized with her own collection of Lemurian crystals that she

had chosen. She had experienced a ritual and had been attuned to the specific energies of these novel crystals by one of the workers. He turned out to be descended from a long line of Medicine Men of the Cherokee Nation. I noticed the time—we'd been there for three hours—and showed Lyn the crystal that wanted to go flying without telling her why. Instantly, she said, "This crystal wants to fly!"

Lyn had picked up one of the crystals to look at and it had "stuck" to her hand. She literally couldn't put it down. That's when she was spirited away by the Cherokee Medicine Man for the attunement; she was also taught how to pass this energy link on to others.

Among the Lemurian crystals we'd chosen, Lyn and I had each selected two for ourselves, one as a personal crystal and the other as a teaching crystal to help in our classes and workshops. The owner then gave us two more, one each to carry with us. He said these would help us to hear each other, and to communicate when we were apart; and they do. In fact, this is not unique to Lemurian crystals. I've found any type of quartz crystal will do this if the crystals are specifically selected with this in mind and it is their sole task.

## the masters

The teaching crystals we'd selected both turned out to be "Master" Russian Lemurian Seed Crystals. Masters were destined to be with people who would teach others. They did the choosing—not us; they picked the people they would work with. Out of all the crystals we selected that day, only three were "Masters". It was as if the "Master" crystals wanted to help find teachers for the crystals' new-found human friends. Neither of us knew who the third teaching crystal would be for; it was a mystery.

We started to pack the crystals for shipping home, and as we were wrapping them, I started to write people's names on the protective packaging of individual crystals. I noticed that Lyn was doing the same. I thought this was odd. We've often been asked to pick a crystal for someone when we've been on buying trips, but this was over a hundred crystals, each destined for an individual person. The owner said these crystals were aiming to place themselves across the world for the benefit of humankind. When we'd finished packing, we didn't know who 16 or 17 crystals were for, and we noticed also that we hadn't packed the crystal that wanted to go flying. We thought that, for whatever reason, it didn't want to come with us and left it behind. We paid for the crystals and left, satisfied with a wonderful morning's work.

The day before we left we went to say goodbye to the Lemurian crystal man. He told us the crystal that wanted to fly had been bought by a pilot! He planned to carry it in his flight case, so it would be flying every few days and sending its positive energy to points around the world. It would also be gridding, or connecting with, the other Lemurian quartz crystals as it criss-crossed the skies.

In England, every crystal found its home. Customers old and new would come into the shop, saying something like, "I just had to come in." When they were shown the Lemurians, every one of them knew immediately why they'd come. But it is still a mystery.

## Chapter 6

# Medicine Bag
# The Psychology of Stones

This chapter explains the tradition of the Medicine Bag

and what could go into yours, how to choose your

stones, how to work with the contents of your

Medicine Bag and refine and enlarge your collection,

revealing how your inner self chooses crystals to

enhance your life without really trying.

# your medicine bag

*Traditionally, a medicine bag is something a person will carry with them; it holds unique items to protect the wearer against all manner of evil spirits and bad luck. It can contain many things, such as ash from a ceremonial fire, feathers, and special herbs, along with small stones and crystals that are meaningful to the wearer. Native American medicine bags are usually compact and made of leather, to wear around the neck, and are kept for a lifetime.*

Another sort of medicine bag is one carried by a healer. Even in prehistoric times, a medicine man or woman might have traveled with the hunters, to give not only practical help but also predictive or intuitive assistance, perhaps by finding the location of a herd of bison. Items from the medicine bag, such as precious stones, could have been laid out and consulted or read. In modern days, the bag a doctor carries with him could be symbolically identified as his medicine bag, as could the paramedic's rucksack. (See page 115 for crystal healing techniques.)

*amethyst*

*snowflake obsidian*

## choosing your bags

*These bags will contain crystals and stones. Various medicine bags can be kept for different purposes. You might have one large bag, several small ones, or even a special box or a large shell or bowl. Any container is fine, so long as it pleases you and is functional. For example, you could have one large bag or box that you keep at home, and transfer selected crystals into a smaller traveling bag when necessary. This could be for a journey across the world or just to the local park.*

Another useful bag would be one for taking to your place of work, containing the crystal "tools" that are most likely to be needed that day. Besides your own stones, these could include any you may want to give to someone who is having problems, say clear quartz for clarity; some to cheer up a sad friend, maybe one with a funny face plus one to create positive feelings, such as an amethyst. Snowflake obsidian to calm a work colleague who is often argumentative and abrasive would be a useful addition—just placing it discreetly nearby will aid any situation that arises by introducing the stone's gentle energy into the area.

My (Lyn's) traveling bag is a small leather pouch with a leather neck cord. I bought it, together with the stones it still contains, many years ago from a Native American Elder in the Arizona desert, near Tucson. The stones are: a piece of turquoise, the traditional traveler's protection stone; a tiny smooth finger of extremely clear quartz, for clarity and energy; a slightly larger fine amethyst of the same shape and brightness, for overall protection and physical and emotional balance, essential if called upon to deal with others' issues. It also promotes good health and increases the vitality and strength of the wearer. Lastly, we come to my ruby crystal, which is very special since it holds many record keepers on one of its surfaces, which are shaped like raised triangles. Record keepers help you access the Akashic records, which are like a library containing all the knowledge and wisdom of the universe, often referred to as the collective unconscious. This stone brings health and great depths of wisdom.

I have another bag, made of soft blue velvet with Celtic swirls printed on it in gold, which I either wear around my neck or suspend from a belt at my waist. The two different positions can be useful if wearing stones to help specific physical areas of the body or the energy chakras (see page 119,) such as malachite for the heart and selenite for the lower back.

My largest bag is circular and embroidered with Chinese designs. I keep a large and varied selection of tried-and-tested crystals in here, which I have accumulated over time. I take this one with me if I

*Lyn's medicine bags*

am teaching or working with clients and feel I may need some help in finding a solution, whether practical or inspirational, and to protect myself from any negative energies that may be around. Some of my creative crystals, such as clear quartz and amazonite, often find their way in here, too. When I am out and about, they are apt to initiate bright ideas for all manner of projects, writing, art, or cookery.

Other small bags of stones are put together to suit the day or event. For instance, I may make up a bag containing a chakra set, or a bag of appropriate stones for a client to work with at home. And I like

*green moss agate*

*aventurine*

## creative crystals

I (Lyn) keep a separate little group of creative crystals by my computer, including celestite for creative expression and clear thought, carnelian to help with study, memory, and inspiration, and pink-banded agate for attention to detail. Next to my easel I have opal for inspiration and hemimorphite for luck and creativity—and rose quartz, which magnifies creativity and imagination, will always be close by. Around the kitchen there are many crystals. My favorites to help with cooking are usually among my collection of crystal rabbits, hares, and owls, who all reside on a shelf above my cookery books. From these I might choose a malachite rabbit to bring calm and balance before baking. If I am experimenting with a new recipe, I choose an owl with tourmaline crystals held within his clear quartz body (tourmalinated quartz, to give him his proper name,) which is good for awareness, new challenges, and creativity—all useful when I am cooking a new dish. I may add a piece of moonstone for a dash of passion. Sometimes I hold one or two crystals or, if I am in the middle of working, just focus on the energy from the whole group. It is surprising what they come up with sometimes!

to keep a store of stones to give away. Aventurine, for example, helps with concentration and nervousness, which might be supportive for someone taking an exam. I always place intent into the stone before giving. Another favorite is hematite, for grounding when a person is feeling scattered or chaotic. Occasionally, a stone from my store finds it way to the base of an ailing tree in the nearby woods; perhaps green moss agate, which is a lovely stone that helps all within the plant kingdom.

## bowls of crystals

Several bowls around our home are filled with multitudes of mixed crystals, This way, there is always on hand a crystal to work with and to help and advise when we need it. These bowls fascinate our visitors. They delve into them, pulling out and exclaiming over this one or that, often not realizing what they are revealing about themselves by their choices. They ask us, "What does this one do? What does that one do?" Looks of amazement are common as the stones always tell the truth!

In a healing room, or even in a business situation, having a bowl of crystals around can be useful. The choice a client makes when invited to pick a crystal provides a little clue to how he or she is feeling and to the underlying cause of any problem, or to what the person's motives may be.

## carrying crystals

I often carry a few crystals in my bra or pocket. It can be useful when traveling, making a hospital visit, working with clients, or entering busy, crowded places to be in close physical contact with the stones' energies. It's great to have crystals for "dark alley" fears and to combat stage fright; also to help with reflecting on deeper matters and to cheer you if you are feeling down. Others can help you to carry out a new or difficult task. I call these my "improvement of skills" crystals.

## healing bags

You could keep all your healing crystals in separate bags. One for physical healing could contain, for example, amethyst for headaches, chrysocolla and copper for arthritis, citrine for nausea, and so on. If you are off to the dentist, perhaps a piece of fluorite would be helpful and comforting. Carry them with you just for the time they are needed, removing or exchanging them as appropriate. Another bag could be for emotional crystal helpers, yet another for spiritual ones, and so on, each set of stones being kept distinct from the others.

*chrysocolla*

*amethyst*

Many crystals are concerned not just with one type of healing, but with physical, emotional, spiritual, and lifestyle issues and dilemmas. They can also work in conjunction with each other, boosting their abilities. You need not carry individual stones for every possible thing, just take time and care in your choice when placing your stones into your bag and be aware of their properties. Do you feel your stones work better together if they are all of one "type," or if they are interacting with each other and bringing different energy angles? Why not experiment? You can always look them up in a crystal healing book, such as *The Crystal Healer*.

*citrine*

*copper*

*rainbow fluorite*

# selecting your stones

*Look at a medicine bag not as containing stones especially for healing the body but also as medicine for the mind, and to help guide your life choices and decisions. Color, feel, shape, size, and weightiness can attract you to stones; also whether they are shiny, dull, or patterned. You may choose different ones at different times and in different ways—eyes shut and randomly, or carefully looking, feeling, and holding, meditating with each crystal. You could dowse, or simply be watchful for the stones that want to choose you.*

There may be some crystals that you don't like much, but be aware that stones know what they are doing and these may be the ones you need at this time—the ones that will help you the most. From time to time, once you have made your choices, check through them all again, or dowse to see if there are any you no longer require, or if there are others you need to add.

If you could lay out a person's stone collection over their lifetime, you could almost, detective-like, discover what their life has been like so far. Their creativity, relationships, strengths, weaknesses, longings, fears, and worries are brought to light. All the human conditions could be visible. To choose crystals for your medicine bag is interesting and reveals a great deal about you. For personal insight, it is a wonderful experience, and one that you can repeat whenever you like by either dipping into your bag or creating a new one. There's no limit to how many bags you put together.

# a choice of crystals

These crystals were selected specifically for someone about to set up as a diagnostic complementary health practitioner. The list is by no means exhaustive; all the stones can be worked with for other problems, and other stones can be chosen for the listed issues. You may find you are drawn to some of these stones, or the areas they represent may resonate with you. These crystals are still in the practitioner's original medicine bag, but everyone is different and your bag will contain your own, unique combination of crystals. Next to each one, we've added the crystal's area of expertise, which qualifies it to be included in this collection.

*pink banded agate*

*jade*

*turquoise*

*smoky quartz*

*fluorite*

*carnelian*

| CRYSTAL | KEY AREA |
| --- | --- |
| Aventurine | endocrine system |
| Citrine | digestive system |
| Pink agate | musculo-skeletal system |
| Pink opal | reproductive system |
| Chrysocolla and malachite | respiratory system |
| Amergreen | lymphatic system |
| Hematite | heart and circulatory system |
| Moonstone | urinary tract |
| Blue tourmaline | nervous system |
| Jade | nervous system |
| Angelite | mental processing |
| Tiger's eye | emotional issues |
| Fluorite | dental problems |
| Blue chalcedony | vision |
| Sodalite | auditory issues |
| Lepidolite | skin |
| Labradorite | spiritual well-being |
| Blue lace agate | home life (also communication) |
| Starry jasper (red jasper with pyrite) | relationships |
| Carnelian | children |
| Lavakite | education |
| Sardonyx | health |
| Crazy lace agate | career |
| Turquoise | travel |
| Rainbow obsidian | animals |
| Rose quartz | love |
| Smoky quartz | spiritual path |

# working with your crystals

*Your stones can help you to release your dormant qualities, talents, and creativity. Engage with them, meditate, be intuitive, listen, see, and feel what they are telling you. They will give you courage and confidence to carry out all manner of things.*

## dipping exercise

This is simple to do, but be aware that this method can have quite profound results at times. Literally, give your medicine bag containing your chosen crystals a gentle shake, then dip your hand in. You may like to pull out one crystal at a time and apply them as your stones for the day (see page 111); or you may prefer to seize a whole handful and lay them out, study them, and give them a thorough reading.

## wellness indicators

Crystals can make extremely good wellness indicators. By dipping into your bag, and allowing your intuition to guide your fingers, you will find that when you check up on the crystal you have chosen, it will reveal something concerning your health. With experience, you will get to know and remember what each of your crystals is for. Particularly, if you select several crystals and read them in conjunction with each other, a pattern may evolve, which could be telling. This need not be alarming; for example, it may just be drawing your attention to the fact that you need to drink more water or to slow down a bit. .

## changing the stones

*As your life moves on, so will your crystal requirements. Remember to check and change you medicine bag crystals every now and again, and make sure that your bag always contains at least one helpful crystal for the moment. Some crystals will stay with you for a lifetime while others will come and go.*

Whenever you are selecting stones to transfer from your main bag or box to your traveling medicine bag, think about your life and what you wish to change or enhance. It may be that you are very happy with every aspect of it, and the crystals you choose will be to maintain the status quo, keep everything positive, and your energy flowing freely. But if you feel some things could be improved, make a list of them and select the most appropriate crystals for you at this time. If you are not sure what these are, dowse for the most suitable crystals, or check in a crystal healing book. Take your time, make your selection, and work with the crystals for a week or so. Then examine them, holding each one to see if you can sense whether you want to keep working with that crystal or select a different one. In time, you will have selected a set that is absolutely right for you.

✳ If you find you have too much time on your hands, or are easily bored or agitated, try working with quartz, citrine, garnet, and spessartine.

*garnet*                    *spessartine garnet*

## practical considerations

When making your selection, also think about what you do on a day-to-day basis.

✳ Perhaps you travel to work along busy highways; crystals that offer protection, such as smoky quartz or tourmaline, would be helpful.

✳ You might visit your sick mother on your way to pick up the children; again, protection crystals would be helpful for you, and a health-enhancing stone, such as an amethyst, for your mom. The giving of a gift, besides the properties of the crystal, will help to bring about a change.

✳ Slip a piece of mookaite into your bag, or pocket, to help you cope with the demands of children.

*mookaite*

✳ If you are surrounded by computers and electronic equipment at work, carry crystals to help with the negative energies they emit. Pietersite can relieve the strain of working at a computer screen. Kunzite, chevron amethyst, and fluorite will all protect you from the effects of the emissions and at the same time strengthen your general health.

*pietersite*                    *kunzite*

✳ If you are trying to lose weight, carry some cassiterite to help curb your appetite. It will also keep you grounded, so you don't feel light-headed.

✳ If you are prone to headaches, carry amethyst, which is a reliable stone to help with this problem, and also gives a boost to your general well-being.

# colors

*Why do we choose particular colors at particular times? Colors can be very evocative, triggering various emotional responses. Some are universally known to excite certain emotions. For example, red is known to have a stimulating effect on the nervous system, causing excitement and positivity, whereas blue has the opposite effect of calming and soothing. This fact is used throughout the commercial world to entice us to buy certain products rather than others.*

In prehistoric times, two colors in particular would have dominated life—dark blue, which signified night, a time of slowing down of metabolic and glandular activity, creating passivity and rest; and yellow, the color of sunlight, which brought an increase in metabolic rate and glandular secretions, facilitating anticipation and activity. For the primitive person, hunting, and being on the attack, was probably balanced by being hunted and on the defensive; and all this activity would have been in the interests of self-preservation.

Certain colors affect us in a personal way. For instance, you may hate green because, as a child, you were forced to wear a vile green jumper. Sometimes, the memory of an instance that provokes a feeling for a color is lost in the subconscious mind. You don't remember why you dislike or love it; you just react to it and the reason for the reaction is deeply hidden in our psyche. We are just aware of either a vague uneasiness or a feeling of pleasure, which is triggered by a particular color our subconscious has registered.

## colors and their meanings

These meanings are commonly recognized. In different cultures, the meanings may vary.

| | |
|---|---|
| Violet | magic, mystery |
| Indigo | intuition, meditation |
| Blue | peace, spirituality |
| Green | nature, fertility, calmness |
| Yellow | happiness, joy |
| Orange | vitality, creativity |
| Red | danger, passion, positivity, courage |
| Black | death, earth, stability |
| Gray | maturity, security |
| White | protection, purification |
| Brown | earth, orderliness |
| Multicolored | possibilities, joy, vision |

## shades of color

Color is light of varying wavelengths. All the colors around us are made up from the primary colors of red, blue and yellow. By mixing these primary colors we obtain the secondary colors, and because there are so many various hues of the primary colors, the secondary colors vary, too. Interpretations of subtle moods and feelings can be defined by your choices of color and their subtler hues.

Red and blue = purple
Blue and yellow = green
Yellow and red = orange

The seven rainbow colors are violet, indigo, blue, green, yellow, orange, and red. Black, gray, white, and brown are considered to be colors, too. Crystals come in many different colors and shades, and a number of crystals are multicolored.

# shape

## geometric shapes and meanings

| | |
|---|---|
| Square | earth, stability |
| Triangle | trinity, such as body-mind-spirit |
| Circle | unity, completeness, sacred space |
| Diamond | clarity, wisdom |
| Oval | fertility, rebirth, new beginnings |

*When you are selecting crystals for your medicine bag, shape is a good indicator to bear in mind. Shapes that fit neatly into the hand, and ones that just feel right, often show that you have chosen well.*

✳ You might have some favorite stones that make you feel you are consulting the wise ones— does one look a little owlish, or remind you of an older, wise person?

✳ Strangely shaped stones that may seem unusual or daring can indicate something new and bold and be thought-provoking.

✳ A comical or sympathetic-looking stone can bring a smile on those darker days, a stone that makes you laugh when you are sad. You could choose one that seems to have a face as long as yours, to mirror you, and remind you that life's just, well, life.

✳ A largish stone, smooth and round, can act as a touchstone, soothing and comforting to stroke.

✳ Crystals have a habit of just turning up and catching your eye. If that happens and one jumps out at you, pop it in your bag.

✳ Stones are directional—they can point to the right road to follow, literally, or show the way to reach your personal aims. Notice the shapes and placement of your stones as you pick out a few and scatter them on the floor.

✳ Does a shape remind you of something or someone: an animal shape, perhaps, or a tool or object that has meaning for you? That stone may provide an insight into what you should be doing with your life.

## size and texture

Size can be indicative of how you are feeling, either about yourself or the world around you. Choosing tiny crystals may show you are feeling small and timid; choosing larger ones may also be a sign of feeling small and timid, in need of protection, or that you are feeling expansive and abundant.

The feeling of a smooth, cool crystal in your hand can be soothing and gentle, whereas a stone with a drusy, crystalline surface, although abrasive, can serve as a wake-up call and help you to focus.

## groups of crystals

Many people, consciously or unconsciously, collect crystals that fit into one category or another, for example, all shiny, all round, all white, all heart-shaped. Others go out of their way not to have any two stones the same. Have you chosen crystals mostly of one type? Are they all a shade of green and all pointed? What does this say about you? In this example, green pointed crystals may suggest that you need to look calmly at a new direction in which to go.

*some of Lyn's collection of heart-shaped crystals and stones*

# predictive stones

*Remember that stones can be predictive and lead you to understand something new about yourself. Choose one on the basis of how you are feeling—uneasy, for example. See which stone you find yourself playing with. Check what this may mean in your crystal book. Do you need protection, an outlet for creativity, or to let go of fear? It is always revealing. Perhaps your stone chose you. In any case, add it to your medicine bag.*

A client once phoned me (Lyn) to say that she couldn't understand why she suddenly kept being drawn to rose quartz and moonstone, two crystals that she had never been particularly fond of before. Over the last few weeks she had been carrying them everywhere she went. I asked if there was a possibility of a new addition to the family. She said certainly not. A day or so later, she came in looking both sheepish and thrilled. She had thought about what I had said and gone for a pregnancy test and, yes, she was pregnant.

*moonstone*          *rose quartz*

## wedding anniversary stones

Many ideas about what gemstones symbolize are tied in with love and marriage. However, there is some debate about the exact nature of the gemstones correlating to each anniversary because of the use of old names translated from ancient texts. This is a traditional list.

| | | | |
|-----|-----------|------|-------------------|
| 1st | gold | 15th | ruby |
| 2nd | garnet | 20th | emerald |
| 3rd | pearl | 25th | silver (jubilee) |
| 4th | blue topaz | 30th ` | pearl (jubilee) |
| 5th | sapphire | 40th | ruby |
| 6th | amethyst | 50th | gold (jubilee) |
| 7th | onyx | 60th | diamond (jubilee) |
| 8th | tourmaline | 70th | sapphire (jubilee) |
| 9th | lapis lazuli | 80th | ruby (jubilee) |
| 10th | diamond | | |

# symbolism of gemstones

*Many people like the idea of celebrating special occasions by wearing or giving gems, which are thought to represent differing values and virtues. For instance, pearls are thought to symbolize purity and innocence, and were often the first jewels bought for a girl. Pearls also represent grace, beauty, and status.*

Diamonds represent pure and unbroken love and are therefore often the first choice for engagement rings and eternity rings. The 'girl's best friend' of one popular song, they also symbolize wealth, intellect, and strength. Additionally, they are believed to heighten spiritual awareness.

Emeralds are associated with love, sensuality, and endurance in a long-term relationship. On another level, they assist with deeper spiritual insights, allowing connection with the divinity within oneself, which leads to kindness, peace, and patience.

It is the combination of you and the stone, not the stone on its own, that is important and often enlightening.

## treasure chest

*In our shop we had a treasure chest that was always filled with tumble stones of all varieties and colors, and we noticed that children were drawn to it like iron filings to a magnet. The preferences of each child were fascinating to observe. Some liked big chunky crystals, while others preferred the tiniest, or perhaps the darkest ones. Many girls picked out all the pink ones. Some children chose each crystal carefully; others picked them up totally randomly. Mostly a pattern would emerge.*

Parents would sometimes try to influence a child's choice and be met with fierce refusals to listen, or tears as the child reluctantly gave in to the adult's selection—"You'd much rather that nice bright blue one than that dull black one, surely?" The grown-up did not realize that the child was drawn to the black one for a reason. Children tend to be instinctive and uninhibited in their choices, and often get it right. We can do the same if we put our intellect to one side for a while and allow our intuition to take over. Other parents, perhaps knowing about the mystic powers of the stones, would be curious to see what was revealed to them about their child's inner nature, character, or sometimes state of wellness. It's fascinating to watch the intense concentration on a child's, or indeed an adult's, face while they choose their stones.

Some people, children and adults alike, prefer to buy bags of mixed stones, trusting the universe to decide for them—a sort of lucky bag, to be dipped into or read and mulled over later, like a Tarot reading.

Some employ the eyes-closed method—grabbing handfuls and not looking until the bag is full to see what they have chosen.

## finding your stones for the day

First thing in the morning, spend some time choosing each crystal to put in your traveling bag. Pick them out one at a time and examine them to see if they are likely to have any significance to you throughout the day you are expecting. Scrutinize them carefully, noting colors, shapes, textures, and anything else about them that may seem relevant. How do they feel? How do they make you feel as you hold each one? Choose as many or as few as you like.

Carry them with you all day and into the evening. At the end of the day, take out your crystals and again examine them carefully, noticing everything about them. Check on their healing qualities and other meanings, if necessary, or meditate with them to find their relevance to the day's events. Is one of them triangular? Perhaps you have been faced with three directional choices, physically or emotionally. A blue stone may have been telling you to calm down a bit, or that it was just the right color for a new sweater you were contemplating buying. The message is not always deep, but just meaningful; sometimes crystals can help with lighter issues, as well as the profound.

If you haven't much time in the morning, dip into your medicine bag as before, and pick out one crystal. Don't look at it but slip it directly into your pocket or bra and carry it with you all day. Follow the above instructions for the end of the day.

## Chapter 7

# An Introduction to Crystal Healing

Crystals have been worked with since the dawn of
time for healing the physical body and bringing
balance to the emotions and the mind. Here we
explore some simple crystal healing techniques, giving
possibilities for you to discover your own path on
your crystal healing journey.

# healing with crystals

*Crystal healing is a method of relieving physical, emotional, mental, and spiritual symptoms by placing crystals, gemstones, rocks, and minerals on or near the body. There are many different ways to do this, depending on culture and belief. Separate crystals can be worked with to energize the healing stones; the divine power of a god or the spirits can be summoned through meditation or prayer to help in the healing process.*

The concept of healing with crystals has been around since the earliest records of humankind, and almost definitely before. For example, it is now believed that the Preseli blue stones used to build the original stone monument at Stonehenge in England around 2150 BCE were chosen and moved more than 200 miles (322km) from a quarry in Wales, specifically because of their special healing powers. Small ones may have been given to people seeking health by the priests. They would then probably have been carried by the seeker; or applied to areas on his or her body requiring

healing, either with the seeker lying down, or by a priest strapping the stones to the body using animal hide and sinew.

Many explanations are offered for how crystals work, from the scientific, linking photons of light and the piezo- and pyro-electric properties of crystals, to the pseudo-new-age, catch-all "through the vibrations." None of them matter. It is the healing effect experienced by so many people who have found improvements of their own conditions, from short-term ailments, such as colds or flu, to long-term chronic illness, that offers proof of crystal healing.

## crystals in your everyday life

Crystals can focus, store, transmit, and transmute energy, and these properties can be demonstrated in your 21st-century life-style.

✳  A CD player has a laser that works by focusing energy to a tiny point. Lasers are mostly red because they use a ruby crystal to focus the energy.

✳  Wristwatches often use quartz because quartz crystal can be made to vibrate at very accurate rates and keep exact time. The crystals store energy and release it, a little like an electrical capacitor.

✳  Have you listened to the radio today, or were you woken by a radio alarm? Early wireless technology that later developed all the way to digital radio was crystal driven. Sound waves are just another form of energy and crystals resonate at a specific frequency, a fact used in the early crystal wireless sets. You can still make them today and kits are often sold in toy shops.

✳  The lighter for your gas barbecue, hob, or cigarette may well use the piezoelectric effect of quartz crystal as its ignition source.

In crystal healing, crystals can focus healing energy on a specific area of the body. They can be programmed by thought, repeated usage, and meditation to store information about how to heal a specific condition. They can transmit healing energy in the case of distant healing, and transmute unhelpful energy into supportive forces within and around us.

# before you start

*It is important to be aware of several things that are relevant to all forms of crystal healing. These are preparing yourself and your space, grounding, selecting your crystals, and cleansing your crystals.*

Some simple things that will help you are: to be clean, focused, and relaxed. Have a shower before you start to wash away any negativity that may be around you. Hold two amethyst crystals, one in each hand. Now, imagine the energy flowing from your right hand to your left, up through your arm, filling your body, then down your right arm into your right hand and back across to your left hand again, until you feel completely focused on the energy flow. Take several slow deep breaths and count to five as you breathe in and out. Holding your amethyst crystals as you breathe deeply will help you to feel more and more relaxed.

## preparing your healing space

Ensure the room you'll be working in is clean and orderly. Place your crystals and stones within easy reach. Cleanse the room, especially if it serves other functions when you are not healing, perhaps as a living or a dining room. There are several methods of doing this, but I like to use a smudge stick in the Native American way, wafting the smoke from a smouldering sage leaf bundle into the corners of the room to drive away unwanted energies and spirits. Ensure the room is warm. You may like to dim the lights or burn a candle and play some relaxing music.

## grounding

*Sometimes, either during or after healing work, you may feel a little spacey. This is nothing to worry about, and the feeling will pass, but if you feel a bit giddy or wobbly, or need to drive, it is always best to ground yourself to stop the sensation.*

### your own experiences

Grounding can relate to the experiences you have and how you integrate them into your life. For example, there are many people who attend healing or new-age workshops, have a great time, feel a sensation, see this angel, or hear that spirit. They go home, tell a friend "who understands these things," and then carry on with their daily lives as if they'd never been. But you can have much more than this just by being grounded. It's a little like having your cake and eating it!

In this sense grounding is bringing whatever you have experienced in the workshop, into your daily life, allowing you to benefit on all levels rather than solely the intellectual. Repeat the two exercises below regularly to ground your experience; or after a workshop, class, or meditation, take a moment and imagine you are a tree and from your feet there are roots growing deep into the ground. When you feel rooted in reality, take your new experience and understanding, and move forward.

1 Hold a hematite stone for a few minutes. Hematite is a naturally grounding crystal and simply by holding the stone or putting it in your pocket or bra, you will find that you feel as if you have your feet back on the ground.

2 Imagine yourself by a river. Picture yourself taking off your shoes and socks and walking on the muddy bank. Feel the mud squelch in between your toes and over your feet. When you are satisfied with this experience, let your imagination go, and bring your senses back to the here and now.

*hematite*

## selecting your crystals

If you know what's troubling or ailing you (or someone else) you can look up a crystal prescription in a crystal remedies guide or ailment directory. You can also be sure that any crystals you are drawn to (see page 111) will be helpful.

We are all individual and our problem may have different causes from another person's even if the symptoms are the same, and for this reason, the most accurate method of selecting your crystals is dowsing (see page 16.) Dowsing has been used for millennia and is ever popular among both professional and lay healers. Crystal healers prefer crystal pendulums because they are both easy to use and the crystal from which the pendulum is made starts the healing process for you.

To select crystals by dowsing, simply hold your dowsing instrument over a crystal and ask, "Is this crystal good for me?" or "Is this a good crystal for my client/friend/relation?" Don't think about it at this stage; just collect up the helpful crystals, make a note of their names—you can look them up later to see how they may help you.

 You can tell physically when crystals need cleansing. They lose their sparkle, look dull, and their colors may even fade. They can also feel slightly sticky or tacky when you hold them.

## cleansing your crystals

Once you have selected your crystals, you will need to cleanse them. This applies whether you are self-healing or healing others. It is necessary because, as crystals work, they pick up energy that is released by the people they are healing—energy that is not needed and may be harmful or restricting. Your crystals will store this "negative" energy and may transmit it to the next person you work with. That's bad! Even a "new" crystal will have collected energy from the miner, shipper, store keeper, and anybody else who may have handled it before it came to you.

*There are many ways to cleanse crystals—you can find them in books and on the internet. Some are simple, others involve complex rituals. Two simple methods that work well are:*

1 Holding your crystal under running water (for crystals that are not water soluble). Hold your crystal in or under a source of water for a few minutes. Some will need more time than others, but you'll soon be able to tell how long each one needs with a little experience. A stream is an ideal water source, but a tap will do fine.

2 Giving your crystals a vacation by placing them on an amethyst or quartz crystal bed. Just like us, your Stone People friends get tired. How long a rest they need depends on how worn out they are. Look at them every few days and sooner or later you'll notice they seem brighter, their colors deeper, and the sparkle returns. You will notice the sticky feeling has gone, too.

# crystal healing techniques

*This is split into three sections. Part 1 is simply holding, carrying and wearing crystals. Part 2 is based around the chakra (human energy) system and rainbow-colored crystals to correlate with the chakras' healthy energies. Part 3 is the application of specific crystal-healing techniques that can work by themselves or be added to the first two parts.*

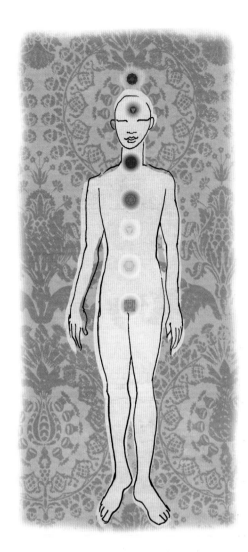

PART 1: Start collecting crystals and stones from shops and shores that you visit. You can find them anywhere. Select one or more crystals from your collection and keep it with you all day and all night. You can put the crystals in your pocket, bra, or a pouch to wear around your neck or on a belt loop, and place them under your pillow, in your bed, or on a bedside table at night. You may find them in the form of jewelry that you can wear; some stones may have a natural hole you can thread a thong through. Try to have as much physical contact with your crystals as you can. Hold them, play with them, meditate with them, and place them near you so you can see them. The more contact you have, the better and quicker they will work.

PART 2: We have seven major chakras, or energy hot spots, in our bodies (see illustration above.) Each chakra is a meeting point of lines of energy running through our bodies and these create a vortex, making them the easiest places for us to exchange energy with the outside world. They draw it in and send it out, and so they are the easiest places to work with crystals to activate the healing process.

Each chakra relates to specific areas of the body, internal organs, and psychological aspects of your life. Your physical, emotional, mental, and spiritual energy goes in and out of balance continuously, like a balance scale finding its point of equilibrium as you add and remove weights. These energy hotspots are the key zones of healing balance, and placing the specified crystal on the chakra, or keeping the stone with you during your day, can help to balance the energy in the chakra, leading to a positive, healthy outlook.

PART 3: These are just a few examples of many crystal-healing techniques:

## quartz crystal for pain relief

1 Hold a clear quartz crystal in your hand with the point directed down.

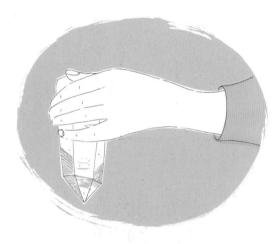

2 Move the crystal in clockwise circles about two inches above any area of pain or discomfort. You will notice that the aches and pains diminish quite quickly and often go completely. Be aware that the discomfort may appear to increase before it gets better. Just persevere—it will improve. You'll also find that working with the same quartz crystal each time will be quicker and more efficient than working with a new one each time.

## energizing quartz crystal

You can move your quartz crystal in the same way over other crystals, including the chakra crystals, to energize them and increase their efficacy.

There is an adaptation of the above technique where you move the quartz crystal counter-clockwise over a particular chakra crystal, to release emotional blocks locked in the chakra. Such emotional blocks are a significant cause of disease that can manifest in physical symptoms, emotional upset, or mental unrest. To clarify these techniques, you can always work moving your quartz crystal in a clockwise direction. If you feel that the person you are healing has emotional needs and is blocked on this level, then work with your quartz crystal in a counter-clockwise direction. You will learn to notice this as you gain more experience, but in the meantime you can ask your pendulum whether you should work in a clockwise or a counter-clockwise direction for each chakra.

*quartz crystal cluster*

*phantom quartz—crystal point with chlorite Phantom*

# chakras and color

Each chakra resonates with a color from the rainbow spectrum.

Crown chakra            violet
Brow chakra             indigo
Throat chakra           blue
Heart chakra            green
Solar plexus chakra     yellow
Sacral chakra           orange
Base chakra             red

Although you can work with any set of crystals in these colors, I find the following selection works particularly well:

Crown chakra            amethyst
Brow chakra             lapis lazuli
Throat chakra blue      blue lace agate
Heart chakra            malachite
Solar plexus chakra     citrine
Sacral chakra           carnelian
Base chakra             red jasper

Now you can begin with the technique known as the Laying on of Stones.

1 Lie down and place each of your chakra crystals on the corresponding chakra.

2 Relax. Stay there for 30 minutes. You may like to use this time to meditate or focus your thoughts on any area of your body or lifestyle that you feel needs a boost of healing energy.

## additional crystals

We are often presented with specific issues from clients, ranging from the obvious and physical to the unspoken emotional. Firstly, this method can help identify unexpressed ailing, and secondly, whether spoken of or not, all diseases are linked and have an energetic cause trapped in the chakra system. By bringing balance to the relevant chakra we can release this trapped energy, restoring health.

Using any of the crystal selection methods described above, choose one extra crystal for each issue. For the purposes of this explanation, we will assume there is only one issue to deal with, although in reality there may be several. With the person in need of healing lying down, place the crystal on the relevant area of the body. If this is for you, you will need to ask a friend to help. Occasionally, the positioning may be obvious, such as a physical injury, but even in this case emotional links are often involved. So whether the area seems obvious or not, I (Philip) always like to dowse with my lapis lazuli crystal pendulum, moving it over the body as if it was divided into a grid format, asking, "Should this extra crystal go here?" and looking for the pendulum's positive response. Once that position is found, it indicates the latitude where the crystal needs to be. I repeat the exercise going across the body from one side to another along this line to find the exact spot.

## amethyst crystal trail

As soon as this extra crystal is placed, it will start working on the issue at hand, but we are looking beyond this to the energetic cause of the ailment, which will be seated in one or more of the chakras. Again, here we'll assume that the source is within only one chakra. You may be able to identify it intuitively, or you can work with your pendulum. Don't rely on logic, such as if the issue is a recurring sore throat, it must be a problem with the throat chakra. That is likely to be wrong.

Once you have identified the chakra, place small amethyst crystals or tumble-polished stones on the body, linking the extra crystal to the chakra concerned, and leave them there for 15 to 30 minutes. During this time, the trapped energy will be released from the chakra, allowing the person to let go of the symptoms and move on with life. Please note that it may take several treatments for all the energy to dissipate.

You can energize all the crystals with your quartz crystal, as described above.

## hand crystals

These are simply reasonably large crystals, often smooth tumble-polished stones, which feel comfortable to hold—not too small and fiddly, but not too big or heavy either. Hand crystals can be beneficial for people with emotional issues, adding an extra calming measure to any treatment. They can also be worked with independently as a treatment in themselves.

In either scenario, I (Philip) place one calming crystal, such as calcite or rose quartz, in each of a client's hands and leave them there throughout the treatment. Other crystals can be substituted, depending on a client's character—a person with his or her head in the clouds needing grounding may benefit from hematite or schorl (black tourmaline); for someone who has been bereaved, smoky quartz or amethyst can to help relieve the grief.

### better and better

Crystals improve the quality of life and increase the speed of recovery from any illness or "dis-ease," be it physical, emotional, mental, or spiritual. They facilitate lifestyle improvements and encourage change, making you a happier, healthier person. It is our experience that whenever someone follows a full course of crystal healing, he or she discovers significant improvements on all levels of well-being.

*red calcite*

*rose quartz*

*green calcite*

*amethyst*

*hematite*

# Useful Resources

You may find the following websites useful:

www.thecrystalhealer.co.uk
For crystals, books, music, and guided meditation CDs and incense.

www.daler-rowney.com
For art materials.

www.geigerminerals.com
For unusual crystals in the USA.

www.paradisemusic.co.uk
For relaxing music and guided meditations on CD.

www.shamanscrystal.co.uk
For crystals and other new-age items.

www.winsornewton.com
For art materials.

## Other books by Philip Permutt
*The Crystal Healer*
*The Complete Guide to Crystal Chakra Healing*
*The Crystal Tarot*

# Index

agate
  Biblical beliefs 88
  blue lace 91, 104, 121
  crazy lace 104
  green moss 100, 101
  pink banded 45, 101, 104
  special stones 35, 36, 45–6
ajoite 78
Akashic records 78, 100
amazonite 100
amergreen 104
amethyst
  chevron 106
  crystal energy 72, 79
  in home 67–8
  qualities 32, 37, 77, 78, 99, 100
  special stones 36, 37, 46
  use in healing 102, 106, 116, 118,
    121, 122, 123
ametrine 71
ancestors 11, 18, 21, 25, 78
angelite 104
animals 42, 77, 78, 101
aqua aura 44
aquamarine 39, 72
Arthur, King 18, 83
astronomical alignments 11, 17, 18
Avebury 11–17
aventurine 72, 74, 100, 101, 104

bears 41, 63
Bible 7, 88
bookends 46, 55
bracelets, Buddha 91
butterflies 41, 71, 87

calcite 7, 78, 123
calmness 35, 36, 37, 39, 78, 93, 101,
  123
Carnac, France 18–21

carnelian 72, 91, 101, 104, 121
cassiterite 106
cave painting 60–1
celestite 78, 101
chakras 7, 17, 100, 119–22
chalcedony 45, 104
change 37, 42, 44, 46, 47, 71, 78
children 67, 106, 111
Christianity 15, 16, 18
chrysocolla 102, 104
citrine 40, 72, 102, 103, 104, 121
clarity 99, 100, 101, 108
cleansing
  crystals 33, 36, 40, 87, 118
  healing preparation 116, 117
color 87, 107, 121
communication 38, 39, 69, 74, 91
compassion 36
compulsive behavior 36
computers 101, 106
concentration 37, 67, 101
copper 102, 103
Cote des Megaliths 18–21
creativity 35, 37, 39, 40, 43, 77, 100–1
crocoite 71
crystals
  alluvial 32
  in bowls 102
  carrying 91, 102, 105–6, 111, 119
  cleansing 33, 36, 40, 87, 118
  collecting/choosing 32–4, 67, 93,
    103–4, 109, 111, 118
  color 87, 107
  crystal grid 76
  directing intent 75
  dowsing 118
  elestial 38, 47
  energy 37, 42, 72, 74, 92, 116
  etched/faden 38
  hand 123

healing 115–23
  Lemurian seed 94–5
  medicine bags 99–106, 111
  meditation 36, 42–3, 69–70, 72, 92
  modern usage 116
  programming 73, 75, 76, 116
  qualities 32–3, 34, 72, 91–3
  rainbow 38, 40, 87
  skulls 84
  special 34–47
  use at home 67–8, 101–2

death 18, 43, 86, 87, 123
diamonds 33, 42, 78, 110
divination 71–2
doorstops 55
dowsing 16, 17, 68, 71, 93, 118, 121
dreams 33, 77–9, 89, 90
Dreamtime 25, 26

Egyptians 7, 43, 51, 86, 87
emerald 89, 110
emotions
  colors 107
  crystals 36–7, 41, 71, 100, 102,
    106
  removing blocks 46, 120, 122–3
energy
  attuning to 95
  crystals 37, 42, 93, 100, 116
  from sun/stones 20
  lines 16, 17
  negative 33, 86, 100, 106, 116, 118
  sensing 72, 74
eudialyte 71

faces 34–7
fairy stones 90
feel better stones 35, 39, 41, 99, 106
femininity 44

flint 32–3
fluorite 41, 78, 102, 103, 104, 106
friendships 54, 78, 93
fulgurite 37

garnet 32, 106, 110
gemstones 33, 110, 115
gifts, leaving 17, 18
gold 110
Greeks 7, 83, 87, 89
grounding 17, 39, 41, 101, 106, 117, 123

healing
  crystals 38–40, 44, 71, 73–4, 84, 87, 89
  holey stones 90
  medicine bags 99, 100, 102–3, 106
  preparation for 115–18
  Stone People 88–9
  symbols 65
  techniques 119–23
health 68, 91, 100, 104, 105, 106
help, asking for 14, 17, 18, 75, 76, 77–9
hematite 17, 101, 104, 117, 123
hemimorphite 6, 35, 101
holey stones 90
home, crystals in 67–8, 101–2

images 22–4, 51–2
indicolite 42
inspiration 37, 38, 40, 45, 46, 77, 101
intuition 36, 90, 99, 111

jade 87, 104
jasper 36, 72, 104, 121
jet 86

Kata Tjuta 26
Kerlescan alignments 18, 20, 21
kitchen crystals 101
kunzite 106
kyanite 71, 78

labradorite 104
landscape painting 62
lapis lazuli 7, 45, 78, 86, 88, 110, 121, 122
larvikite 78, 104
Lemurian seed crystals 94–5
lepidolite 104
luck 35, 84, 85, 87, 90, 99, 101

malachite 35, 78, 100, 101, 104, 121
medicine bags 99–106, 111
meditation
  crystals 36, 42–3, 69–70, 72, 92, 106
  holey stones 90
  painted stones 55–6
  walking 21
Merlin 18, 83
message stones 53, 55
metamorphosis crystals 37, 44, 87
meteorite 42
mind 37, 41, 43, 101
moldavite 78
mookaite 106
moonstone 75, 101, 104, 110

Native American beliefs
  crystal attunement 95
  gifts 18
  healing 99, 100, 117
  Heart-line Bear 63
  Sonoran Desert 22, 23
  Stone People 7, 88–9
  talking stick 38
  turquoise 87

obsidian 78, 99, 104
Odin stones 90
Olga, Mt 26
onyx 110
opal 84–5, 101, 104

pain 73–4, 100, 102, 106, 120
painting stones
  choosing rocks 52–4
  equipment 57–8
  inspiration 55–6
  projects 58–63
paperweights 54, 55, 59
parking space 75, 76
peace 37
pearls 110
pebbles 31–4, 51–63
perception 90
petroglyphs 22–4
physical boost 36, 68, 100, 106
pietersite 106
plants, ailing 76, 101
positivity 37, 38, 99
predictions 71–2, 99, 110
pregnancy 110
problem solving 12, 14, 43, 70
protection
  crystals 36, 38, 39, 41, 45, 47, 86, 87
  holey stones 90
  medicine bags 99, 100, 106
  personal space 67–8
psychic abilities 43
pyramids 43
pyrite 67, 104

quartz
  blue 42
  crystal grid 76
  directing intent 75
  elestial sheet 47

energizing crystals 120
fulgurite 37
healing 39, 73, 89, 120, 123
Lemurian seed crystals 94–5
manifestation egg 41
metamorphosis 37, 44, 78, 87
modern usage 6, 116
properties 87, 89, 99, 100, 101, 118
rose 77, 78, 101, 104, 110, 123
smoky 38, 47, 67, 78, 93, 104, 106, 123
spheres 47, 89
talking 38
Tibetan 38, 47

rainbow 38, 40, 87, 107
record keepers 100
Reiki 42
relationships 35, 45, 54, 110
rivers 12, 14, 32
rock art 48–63
Romans 15, 18, 51
ruby 33, 78, 89, 100, 110, 116
rutile 41

sacred sites 6–7
  Avebury 11–17
  Cote des Megalithes 18–21
  Sonoran Desert 22–4
  Uluru 24, 25–7
  use by other religions 15, 18
sapphire 45, 88, 110
sardonyx 104
schorl 39, 123
selenite 100
shape 41, 108–9
shock, delayed 44
silver 110
sleep 47, 78, 79
smudge stick 117

sodalite 104
solstices 17, 18
Sonoran Desert 22–4
South America 84, 87
spessartine 106
spheres 46, 47, 89
spirit guides 12, 41, 43, 55
spirituality 36, 38, 41, 43, 78, 87, 90, 102
standing stones 11–21, 73, 92
Stone People 7, 33, 69, 74, 87, 88–9, 118
Stonehenge 7, 73, 115
stones
  asking for help 17, 18, 75, 76
  collecting 6, 31–4, 52, 67, 103
  connecting with 14, 21, 111
  entering 13
  finding 32–4
  friendship 54
  healing 90, 115
  with holes 90
  leaving gifts 17, 18
  negative energy 33, 118
  painting 51–63
  power of 12, 67, 73, 83–4, 92
  special 34–47, 63, 88
  spirit 84–7, 88
  tumble-polished 32, 72, 111, 123
stress 37, 41
studying 101
sun, welcoming 20
symbolism 110

talking 38, 46, 71
teaching 39, 46, 95
teamwork 78
Ten Commandments 88
texture 109
Tiger's eye 104

topaz, blue 110
tourmaline 106, 110
  black (schorl) 39, 123
  blue 42, 104
  in quartz 101
  rods 47
  watermelon 41
transformation 41, 42
traveling stones 87, 92, 100, 102, 105–6, 111
truth 38, 93, 102
turquoise 78, 87, 100, 104

Uluru 24, 25–7
universe, connecting 24, 42
uvarovite 32

walking 21, 26
wedding anniversaries 110
weight loss/gain 40, 106
wisdom 100, 108
wood, fossilized 41, 86
workplace 99, 102, 106

## Authors' note

Some of the designs, ideas, and symbols that we have used in this book hold deep meaning or are considered sacred within certain cultural contexts. Please respect them as we do and accept that they are reproduced in true faith to their original intent. We really appreciate the local indigenous people we have met on our travels and their sharing of their traditions, beliefs, and world view.

## Picture credits

Used under licence from Getty, 2011:
p25 © John W Banagan; p30 Don Smith

Used under licence from iStockphoto, 2011
p23 © Ken Canning

Used under licence from Shutterstock, 2011:
p6 © Marcin Ciesielski / Sylvia Cisek; p10 Matthew Collingwood; p19 © Fred Goldstein; p27 Edella; p33, bottom right, © nadi555; p50 © Victoria Field; p82 © Stock Cube; p86, bottom left © Nadi555

p84 © The Trustees of the British Museum

Copyright Ryland Peters and Small
p2 Paul Manning; p66 Polly Wreford

## Acknowledgments

We would like to thank each other for the love and support through the creative period of this book. To have one author entrenched in front of a computer is one thing, to have two is quite another! Thanks also go to our friends and family, for their understanding and patience as we methodically ignored them while writing this book.

Lyn would like to thank her son Roy and grandson Jay for just being themselves and to whom the future belongs. She also thanks her dearest friend, Joan, who has been the best rock anyone could have, keeping Lyn steady over years too many to mention with her kindly wisdom and pithy humor.

Our thanks also go out to all the people at CICO Books who have helped with this project, especially to Cindy Richards for her continued faith.

A big thank you must also always go to all our students and clients who inspire and bring this book to life. They provide the questions that spur our quest on and often the answers, too.

And, finally, to Philip's father, Cyril, who inspired him in life and continues to inspire from the afterlife, and Ian, who still knows why.

LYN PALMER & PHILIP PERMUTT
MARCH 2011

Contact:
Philip Permutt at www.thecrystalhealer.co.uk
Lyn Palmer at lynpalmerart@yahoo.com